THE HEART OF A BEAST

Mrs cayon
You are such a
Beast! keep Doing
What you do.

SURVIVING IN THE LONE-WOLF ECONOMY

THE HEART OF A #BEAST

LONNIE GORDON OGULNICK

THE HEART OF A BEAST
Surviving in the Lone-Wolf Economy

ISBN 978-1-61961-546-5 *Paperback*
978-1-61961-547-2 *Ebook*

For my wife, Dara, who gave me the time away on the weekends to write and who always sees the positive in every situation. For my two daughters, Leah and Ella, who tackle every challenge head-on and light up every room they walk into with positive energy.

CONTENTS

Every year for the last ten years, I made it a tradition to ask one of the world's greatest entrepreneurs for a quotation to live by. This year, Dr. Phil Frost said to me, "Lonnie, believe in yourself and invest in yourself. The rest is in the details."

THE MAN IN THE ARENA

It is not the critic who counts; not the man who points out how the strong man stumbles, or where the doer of deeds could have done them better. The credit belongs to the man who is actually in the arena, whose face is marred by dust and sweat and blood; who strives valiantly; who errs, who comes short again and again, because there is no effort without error and shortcoming; but who does actually strive to do the deeds; who knows great enthusiasms, the great devotions; who spends himself in a worthy cause; who at the best knows in the end the triumph of high achievement, and who at the worst, if he fails, at least fails while daring greatly, so that his place shall never be with those cold and timid souls who neither know victory nor defeat.

THEODORE ROOSEVELT, EXCERPT FROM THE SPEECH "CITIZENSHIP IN A REPUBLIC," DELIVERED AT THE SORBONNE, IN PARIS, FRANCE, ON APRIL 23, 1910

PREFACE

Individualism is freedom, the free will to make decisions that—for better or for worse—fall on your shoulders. When our decisions are good, we get rewarded; when they are not, we still get rewarded. Knowledge is the reward for mistakes made and lessons learned.

The beasts in life take individual freedom and they run with it. They run with intense passion and daggerlike focus, creating in their wake a long line of followers and friends who want to be close in order to learn from them. Along the way, enemies pop up as well, both within and without. The game is a serious one; it is called the game of life. We can choose a life of ease or one of struggle, but both will have their challenges and ups and downs.

We search for answers. My philosophy is that you are either part of the solution or part of the problem. Those who look for solutions are the ones you want on your team because they lift you up when you are down and help you find the answers you are looking for. You'll inevitably deal with those who are part of the problem; try to convert them to be solution-oriented people, or remove them from your life so they can't inflict damage on you.

This book should serve as a guide. I am, like you, a work in progress. I am a soldier on the frontlines dealing with life's daily battles. I strive to improve myself and get better, smarter, and stronger each day. I am on team "blue beast," wanting every day to be filled with a beautiful blue sky under which I look at the world clearheaded, humble, and grateful.

As I look back at my life, I've experienced some minor successes. Many goals I wrote down fifteen to sixteen years ago have been attained, one of which was to write a book. I told myself if I was ever able to give back and help even just one person in life, I would. This book contains some of my knowledge gained from the frontlines, presented in real talk. I am not a writer, a professor, or a historian. I am a lone wolf, and through hard work, perseverance, and lifelong relationship building, I have gained some insights into how this game we call life is played. I don't have all the answers, and I don't know if what I say is right for you, but this is what has worked for me. In addition, I have also reached out and interviewed several entrepreneurial beasts to gain further insight into what makes certain people tick and operate at such a high level. If one sentence from this book moves you in a direction of self-improvement, inner peace, and happiness, then I did my job.

Now grab a few highlighters and a pen or pencil, and fill this book with notes and highlights. Good luck in all you do, and be a beast.

INTRODUCTION

WHAT IS A BEAST?

"Winning is not everything, wanting to win is."

VINCE LOMBARDI

You've most likely heard the term "beast mode" used by sports aficionados regarding former Seattle Seahawks running back Marshawn Lynch. Lynch was nicknamed "a beast" for his aggressive running style and his ability to break multiple tackles and to fly by or run over defenders. By entering beast mode, Lynch contributed greatly to the Seahawks' Super Bowl win in 2013, becoming a legend on the gridiron and subsequently ingraining the word *beast* in every person who watched him. Lynch was operating in the zone—physically and mentally. "Stay in your lane" was a phrase he often used, which referred to his job and staying completely focused on the task at hand. He concentrated his energy on the game and performing at his maximum potential. Nowadays, you'll hear people use the phrase a lot in referencing intense athletes, bodybuilders, or anyone killing it at the gym.

The term goes well beyond sports, though, and we're all capable of being beasts in every aspect of our lives. Entering beast mode is a daily battle of making good choices that propel you forward. Once you conquer these little battles and reap the rewards, entering beast mode becomes an addiction and, with enough practice, a powerful mind-set.

Well before Lynch ever stepped foot on an NFL football field, I first heard someone being referred to as a beast when I was thirteen years old on the wresting mats. I heard it again in 1998 when I started out in finance. The financial world is littered with beasts. Whether it was an advisor with a major wire house, a banker at a regional bank, an independent advisor, or an investment banker logging an insane amount of hours, almost every driven person I met succeeded because of a work ethic that was at such a high level of intensity, it was mind-blowing. When a human operates at extreme levels and has an immensely high work ethic, it's as if he has transformed himself from a human into a machine. Urban Dictionary defines the phrase *beast status* as follows: "When referring to a person, beast status is achieved when the aforementioned person is so good at a certain skill that he has exceeded human comprehension, thus making him non-human." I define it like this: A beast is an attitude. It's discipline. It's entering each daily battle with every ounce of fight you can possibly muster. It's giving that extra drop of blood, extra bead of sweat, and extra ounce of energy when you want to quit. It's running the extra mile, getting up when you get knocked down, and hitting the pillow every night knowing you gave that day everything you had.

A beast is "in the zone" all day; you can sense it and see it, even as an outsider. That superfocused guy at the gym who is in great physical shape ignoring those around him is a beast. He's there for the sole purpose of getting the most out of his workout, whether he's 125 pounds soaking wet or 350 pounds of shredded muscle.

A beast is focused on achieving the impossible. She has committed her mind-set to pushing herself to her maximum potential. An individual who ignores the various little annoying disruptions that pop up throughout the day is in beast mode, totally focused on the task at hand.

To me, most mothers—my wife included—are beasts. When you have a dedication to your child and you put your child above all else, by virtue you will be working harder and longer. Parenthood in general is a challenging journey. A mother beast always does the right thing for her child. Some mothers have to work in addition to raising a family. These mothers don't shy away from what needs to be done and will ruthlessly tackle every obstacle to find a way to make ends meet and care for their children. These women, without a doubt, are 100 percent beast.

Being around others in beast mode will help you get there. Beasts don't hold grudges or make others feel bad when they don't perform to their best ability, either. They understand that it's a daily struggle and that sometimes, even in a victorious war, everyone loses a battle here or there. Beasts encourage and inspire; you want to surround yourself with them because you'll rub off on each other, leading to positive growth. When you're a beast, people gravitate to you because they feed off of your infectious energy and want to be around it. You'll want to be around people who are focused and have their shit together, too, because you want to gain knowledge from them. You want to figure out what they are doing that makes them so successful.

IT'S NOT JUST ABOUT THE MONEY

Being a beast isn't just about making a lot of money. Tapping into your inner beast can help you prosper in multiple areas of your life—relationships, health, career, sports, love.

It's about being passionate and excelling at whatever you put your mind to. Take my daughter's soccer coach, for example. This woman doesn't make a lot of money, but she puts everything she has into coaching a group of excited little girls. She puts a great amount of energy into her kids, to coaching, to the game, and she clearly doesn't do it for the paycheck. Those who take time to share their passion and knowledge with others for nonmonetary rewards are beasts. There are schoolteachers all over the country who don't make as much money as they should, but their students motivate them so forcefully that they strive to give more to them than they might get out of the job monetarily. Teaching and helping kids is their passion. Money isn't the main motivator, so these teachers are beasts because they've committed themselves to being the best teachers they can be.

You may find making a lot of money motivating, and that's fine. Career choice, however, is irrelevant in terms of becoming a beast. What matters is finding what motivates you to push yourself to your highest potential. Entering beast mode and staying there is not temporary—at least is doesn't have to be. It's a lifestyle that becomes who you are.

We all want to be the light in a dark room. When you walk into a dark room, you need to find an outlet and plug into it, lighting up the room. If you don't have an outlet to plug into in your life, you're going to be lost in the dark. You might feel a lack of confidence, a bit uncertain even, and anxiety may hit you. The moment you're able to plug into something, you've tapped into your life's purpose.

How do I take my first step toward finding my purpose?

What do I want to do today, tomorrow, a year from now, ten years from now?

These are questions you should always be asking yourself.

Some people find their purpose fairly easily, but the reality is that most of us don't. Beasts push themselves out of their comfort zone in order to find that purpose, and even when they find it, they continue to push themselves to learn, grow, and overcome fears and challenges. Beasts are a constant work in progress. As we age, our purpose in life will alter and change. There is no such thing as a "final destination"; it's a continual process.

As one New Year started, I began challenging myself and doing things I absolutely detested—yet understanding the potential benefit it would have on me. As my body began to ache and feel more pain due to the different sports I've played throughout my life, I learned about the healing powers of daily cold plunges. A year ago, you couldn't give me a thousand dollars to plunge into in an ice-cold body of water. Just the thought of sitting in freezing-cold water was pure torture—probably one the worst things you could ever do to me because I feared it. Instead of avoiding it, however, I used my fears to push myself, overcome a challenge, and face it. The first day was the hardest, but after a year or so, I now look forward to it and find it an integral part of my day. It still sucks to be in a frozen body of water, but the rewards throughout the day are indescribable. It's amazing what a simple cold plunge can do to your body, mind, and soul. Beginning each day by first confronting and conquering a challenge makes the rest of my day seem a bit easier.

Pushing yourself as a beast is more important than ever because the economy is constantly changing around us, and most—if not all—of it is out of our control. We live in a world with more emphasis on individual effort, less guaranteed security, and higher rewards for winners, so entering beast mode is of utmost importance if you want to survive.

Tapping into your maximum potential might sound like a high standard, but it's something you *can* achieve—and it all starts in the mind. As humans, we all have brains that essentially function the same. Sure, some might have a higher IQ, or others might have a particular disposition to math or music, but if you push your mind and you focus with laser-like intention, you *can* achieve anything.

You won't achieve a goal if you don't have one, however, and a goal is useless unless it has been defined. Therefore, to achieve your goal, you must first define it, and then start moving. It starts with getting out of bed and moving in the direction you want to be heading. Once you're up and buzzing with purpose and momentum, you've entered the "beast mode" mind-set. Straight out of the gates, when you get up in the morning, that battle of waking up or staying in bed is the first choice we make as beasts. Who wins that battle? A close friend of mine who wakes up at 4:45 a.m. has a trick. He places his alarm somewhere he cannot lean over and hit snooze, which forces him to get up and out of bed to shut it off.

For this book's purpose, I break the "beast" concept down into a battle between your internal blue beast and your internal red beast; the blue beast is your partner, and the red beast is your own personal enemy. The blue beast is the good beast. What is beautiful in life? The blue ocean, the blue sky, beautiful blue eyes—I associate blue with beauty. The daily goal is to feed your internal blue beast. You have to give it a lot of food and energy; otherwise, you're going to succumb to that lazy, irritable, nasty red beast we all have within us.

THE IMPORTANCE OF SELF-MOTIVATION

Ask yourself the following questions:

- ☞ **What am I doing in the morning?**
- ☞ **Am I springing out of bed or hitting snooze?**
- ☞ **Am I drinking coffee for a quick energy boost?**
- ☞ **Am I hitting the gym or doing something to get my blood flowing?**
- ☞ **Am I spending an hour in bed on Facebook or social media?**

Your entire day is dictated from the first half hour to hour of waking up, so choose wisely.

Many people settle for mediocrity and don't achieve the things they want in life. You are unaware of the power you have within yourself to achieve anything you want. And you *can* achieve it. This book is here to help.

The path to beasthood takes a lot of work, so it's important to write down where you want your life to go. You control that lever. I truly believe in the power of the pen— once written down, fuzzy thoughts become firm.

Everyone will have different motivations. Personally, the commitment to become a beast came from a dark period in my life. I was lost and I had no direction, but I wanted to be somebody who was successful. I hated losing and was stuck at the bottom for a long time. Today, my motivation comes from the necessity to provide for my family and to help others by sharing some of the knowledge I've gained over the past twenty years on the frontlines of Wall Street.

A lot of successful people overcame dark periods, which propelled them into becoming beasts. As unfortunate as some situations and circumstances can be, they can also be powerful motivators. I encourage you to take any unfortunate experiences, turn them around, and use them as motivation to create a better future for yourself. Many of the most successful people started out in a broken place, often sleeping on friends' couches or starting businesses out of their garages. One trait these people shared was they refused to give up, eventually conquering their adversity.

Take Abraham Lincoln, for example. Despite various business failures, personal loss, rejection, and great financial challenges, Abraham Lincoln became the president of the United States. Lincoln faced many obstacles, both political and private, but overcame them because he had the belief and the determination to never give up. Lincoln is well known for his endurance in the face of adversity. President Roosevelt once said that Lincoln's life "preeminently and distinctly embodied all that is most American in the American character...not the doctrine of ignoble ease, but the doctrine of the strenuous life." Consider the numerous political and personal challenges Lincoln confronted in his lifetime. He ran for the legislature in Illinois and lost; he ran for Congress and lost; he fell in love with a woman, asked her to marry him, and then she died; he ran a business with a partner and, when it failed, spent the next seventeen years paying off debts; he later proposed to another woman, and she rejected him; and that's just to name a few of his hardships! Throughout his life, Lincoln worked in various fields of work, including as a store clerk, soldier, store owner, election clerk, postmaster, state legislator, lawyer, congressman, and, finally, the president of the United States.

Life's hardships are inevitable, and it's okay to be down, to experience low moments, and to have challenging experiences because this is where the motivation to change your life can come from.

ESTABLISHING YOUR VISION

Take a moment right now to reflect on your life. Put pen to paper and write out your vision—what you want from life. If you want to have some fun with this, create a vision board by cutting out pictures and pasting them on poster board. Find a quiet place where nobody can bother you, and take an hour or two (or however long) and really dig deep. Look at your life and identify the reality of where you are right now and where you want to be. Write down your answers to the following questions.

☞ When in life was I the happiest?

☞ When did I overcome adversity?

☞ Who do I look up to or admire?

☞ What positive traits from these individuals do I like? (These traits will give you an outline as to what your potential inner beast is.)

☞ Who or what distracts, destroys, and saps my energy?

☞ What am I unhappy about? (Think of people and/or places you feel are negatively impacting your life right now. Immediately begin extracting everything negative from your life.)

☞ **How can I change that?**

☞ **What's my passion?**

☞ **What's my dream life?**

Write all of your thoughts, feelings, and desires down. Writing these down is the single most important step you can take to make them a reality.

Operating in beast mode, Mark Zuckerberg left college and created a vision for himself and for his business. He could have sold his company for a billion dollars to Yahoo, but that wasn't his goal or his vision—it wasn't about the money for him. He wanted something else, and now the guy's one of the most successful people in the world.

ESTABLISHING YOUR GOALS

Once you've established a vision, start breaking down how you're going to achieve that vision by setting goals. When I started setting goals at the age of twenty-two, I achieved more in that first year than I did at any point in my life prior. Break down your vision into realistic and achievable goals. Be sure to include some wild and crazy goals, too; have fun with it. When you look back at them in ten years, you may surprise yourself.

☞ **Start with a thirty-day challenge. In one month, I will...?**

☞ **My one-year goals are...**

☞ **My five-year goals are...**

☞ **My ten-year goals are...**

Before you start your day each morning, write out the goal for that day and cross it off at night. What do you have to do every day in order to fulfill your vision?

You should have multiple goals in different areas of yo life. Set some career-related goals. What do you want out of work? Do you want to advance in the current company you're working for? How will you do that? Do you want to quit your job and start your own company? Perhaps your goal is to work for your current employer for five years in order to save money so you can start your own business.

Set some relationship-related goals. If you're single and you'd like to get married one day, that's a perfectly acceptable goal to write down. If you have a family, perhaps you would like to spend more time with your kids. Write down how you could achieve that goal. Perhaps it's to create "family-fun nights" every Tuesday where your family plays board games or goes on a hike. These are small, achievable goals you can work toward on a weekly basis.

Set some health-related goals. Do you want to lose weight? If so, how many pounds? Give yourself a goal weight and then start breaking down how you're going to achieve it. Maybe you want to run a marathon or compete in a triathlon. In order to achieve these goals, they need to be broken down into smaller daily and weekly goals for you to focus on.

By creating a vision and then breaking it down into little goals, you're building the road map for your life, creating the life you want. Along your journey, there will be multiple setbacks; embrace them. Failures are opportunities to learn and grow, so don't beat yourself up too much, because they are an important part of the process. As long as you continue heading in a direction that aligns with your mission statement and you put in the work and effort, you're golden.

ESTABLISHING YOUR "WHY"

Creating your vision of who you want to be and breaking that down into smaller, achievable goals is the greatest asset you can have. The next step in the process of becoming that person is to establish your "why." Why are you trying to achieve this vision? Why are you reaching for those goals? Your "why" needs to be powerful because you will return to it repeatedly throughout your journey in becoming a beast. Your "why" will function to keep you on track when you feel defeated or weak. You will undoubtedly have bad days, and returning to your "why" will help you overcome them. You really have to dig into your "why"—and don't forget to write it down.

Your passion is important because when you believe in something with all you have, it will be tough to stop you. Combining your "why" and passion is a key component of becoming a beast.

The vision, the goals, and the why mean absolutely nothing

without action. After you've established them and have written them down, it is time to put in the work—and it's a day-to-day battle. Feeding the blue beast and battling that red beast is a daily struggle, and it's easy to get off track, but that's when you have to refocus. Try going back to the gym or returning to that diet after taking two weeks off—it's hard. The core of this book is about getting your mind right. Once you have your vision, your goals, and your mind motivated to achieve greatness, plus the ability to put in the work, everything starts falling into place. When you're in the mind-set of a beast, you take the reins of leadership, and you begin the journey of creating your own destiny.

Entering beast mode is never-ending, so be prepared to work. Becoming a beast means having scars on your back from going through the trenches of life and fighting the good fight, battle after battle. There is no magic formula. You're going to lose some, but even with some setbacks, it's about making progress and enjoying the journey, not just the destination. You're a work in progress, and you should always be looking for ways to improve. The only time you stop improving is when you allow the red beast to take over. Every day is a battle to wake up and roll that boulder up the mountain. Entering beast mode is a personal journey, and in the following chapters, I'm going to break down the most important aspects of life and help you tap into your inner beast—from the physical to the social to the spiritual.

INTERVIEW WITH PEDRO VALENTE

With a wrestling background and a love for the sport of mixed martial arts (MMA), the Ultimate Fighting Championship was always a stay-at-home night with popcorn in hand. I dabbled in and out of a couple of MMA gyms while working in New York, but suffered a bad rib injury just before moving to Florida. Once I got to Florida—about ten years ago now—I decided to hang up the MMA gloves and pick up a tennis racket. Every now and then, I noticed a training studio called Valente Brothers Jiu-Jitsu in my neighborhood. The thought of returning to the mats was always in the back of my head, and although I was tempted on a few occasions, I never did. While on a ski trip with a close friend, I mentioned this desire to him. Little did I know that Steve had already been training there. When I told him I noticed Valente Brothers Jiu-Jitsu in my neighborhood, he turned to me and said, "Do you have any idea what you have in your backyard? The Valente Brothers are some of the greatest jiu-jitsu self-defense practitioners in the world. They literally trained in the home of Hélio Gracie," the father of Brazilian jiu-jitsu.

I had no clue.

It was all I needed to hear, and upon returning to Miami,

I signed up the next day. The beauty of this academy is the discipline and structure. Even if I wanted to test my skills and spar, I would need to go through a thorough fundamental training in order to get to the advanced classes. Sparring is when the professors think you have mastered the fundamentals of the self-defense fighting system. Injury prevention is one of their primary concerns. You are learning a martial art, which is literally an art of war.

Valente Brothers Jiu-Jitsu is unlike any other academy I have been to; it's serious, but also immensely fun. The three brothers—Pedro, Gui, and Joaquim—are in the process of building a jiu-jitsu mecca in North Miami that will be a world-renown academy, teaching the art of self-defense the way it was meant to be taught. The Valente brothers have a special power, one that you only understand after training under them; you can sense it on your first encounter. Miami is lucky to have adopted them from Brazil.

Here's some more background: The Valente brothers' excellent instruction skills combined with their technical fighting styles allowed them to receive their black belts directly from grandmaster Hélio Gracie. In 1999, Pedro successfully completed the jiu-jitsu professor's course and received his diploma and title of jiu-jitsu professor. In 2001, Gui was also awarded the coveted professor's diploma. This was a great accomplishment and honor in light of the fact that in seventy-five years only twenty-seven people received this diploma from grandmaster Hélio Gracie. The youngest of the Valente Brothers, Joaquim, is also a recipient of the black belt and professor's diploma by grandmaster Hélio Gracie.

I had the privilege to interview the gentle warrior and absolute beast, Pedro Valente, a man I am lucky to call my professor and friend. You would never know it, but all three brothers are walking lethal weapons, the true definition of "heart and beast."

LO: *When did you start training in jiu-jitsu?*

PV: Before I could walk. It is part of my fabric. It's been part of my life ever since I can remember—something my father did and my grandfather did.

LO: *What does jiu-jitsu mean to you?*

PV: It applies to everything, not just fighting. It is a way of life based on efficiency, flexibility, discipline, and overcoming any fears through mental fortitude and courage.

LO: *Are you born a beast, or is it something you can nurture?*

PV: First, I would say it is something you can nurture. We learned this from my father. Success requires work, so he would say, "If you want to be better, you have to exercise and you have to eat. Things don't just come, they come as a result of hard work." He instilled this work ethic in us from an early age and taught us the value of putting the time in. There are no shortcuts.

Now, there are two elements. We are born with our DNA, our genetic code, transmitted from our ancestors, but that does not define us. This gives us a potential. You can be at your highest potential or your lowest potential. Some people say you can't teach heart. I disagree. I think people may be more inclined to being tougher than others, but there is still a potential or a spectrum you are born with. The difference is work—smart, efficient work. I do believe you can teach people to be courageous and tough. So, yeah, it would be both.

LO: *Do you ever find yourself not working up to your potential on the spectrum?*

PV: Yes, absolutely. My own greatest personal enemy is laziness. There is sometimes a tendency to want to rest; you tell yourself you're tired, but you have to fight that! I do believe my greatest enemy is not outside; its inside. [*This is the idea of blue beast versus red beast we discuss in the book.*] I work very hard to identify my personal weaknesses and flaws and make sure I can defeat them.

LO: *To me, you always seem so calm and level. Do you ever lose your temper?*

PV: I do, but because of jiu-jitsu, it is not often. If you asked me ten years ago, I would say I lost it more than I do now, and I hope in ten years from now I can say I lose it even less. But I think I have been improving through this philosophy of jiu-jitsu and also maturing and understanding life. When I do, I try to immediately recognize it. I don't like it, so I try to control it. The best technique is not reacting too quickly. Be silent. Don't speak, even if you think it's important; wait two hours or a day. Give yourself time before you react.

LO: *How many hours of sleep do you get per night?*

PV: Eight hours is important to me, but I don't always get it. It is something that requires discipline as well. I try to take a nap after lunch because I work with my body and I work late hours. I aim for twenty to thirty minutes, but I don't always have the time. I'll set an alarm on my phone for seven minutes though, and I'll fall asleep and wake up fresh, ready for the rest of the day.

LO: *What's your favorite book?*

PV: The first book that comes to mind is *Art of War* by Sun Tzu. In many ways, it defines the philosophy of jiu-jitsu. A close second would be *Healing Back Pain* by Jon Sarno. I have had multiple herniated disks and lots of pain, and that book saved me. It talks about the mind-body connection; it's very powerful.

LO: *Growing up in Brazil, you have crossed paths with many beasts. Who comes to mind when I say the word* beast *and why?*

PV: My father, Pedro Valente Sr. [*one of a few, select grandmasters awarded a Gracie jiu-jitsu red belt*], and my teacher, Hélio Gracie [*who founded with his brother, Carlos, the art of Gracie jiu-jitsu and who founded Brazilian jiu-jitsu*]. My father was physically strong, mentally tough, always true to his principles, and always willing to sacrifice for us. His commitment to his kids and his love was strong. I appreciated his serious approach to our education. The best way to describe him was he had intensity in everything he did.

Hélio Gracie should be in the dictionary under the word *courage*. He jumped from a ship into shark-infested waters to save a man from drowning after the crew had already given up on saving him. He saved the man's life. When he was forty-five years old, a twenty-six-year-old student of his who outweighed him by fifty pounds challenged him to a fight after a falling-out. They fought for three hours and forty-five minutes with no rounds. He defined what courage is. He was always willing to show people how jiu-jitsu was so effective.

LO: *What was the best fight you ever saw?*

PV: Royce Gracie versus Dan Severn. I was there, next to the cage in 1994. It was great because it was the essence of jiu-jitsu. Dan Severn was a beast—an Olympic-caliber, heavyweight wrestler, eighty pounds heavier than Royce Gracie. Royce forced Dan to tap with a triangle choke, putting Brazilian jiu-jitsu on the map as the premier fighting system.

LO: *Do you ever eat pizza or junk food? Do you drink alcohol?*

PV: Yes, I eat pizza. I don't consider pizza to be junk food. I would not eat it if I thought it was bad for me. I don't eat anything that I think is bad for me. I have no cheat days. My diet is based on three concepts: food selection, food combining (organizing your food in a way that is efficient for digestion), and meal spacing. I believe in three meals per day with at least four and a half hours in between. Two of those meals should be fruit-based only, and one cooked meal per day. The main point is conscious nutrition. Eat what you believe is good for you. If you talk about being a beast, it has to be in everything you do. If you eat food you know is bad for you, then that is weakness. I don't want to train to be weak. I never tried a soft drink in my life. I never tried alcohol in my life. I never tried any drugs. I never tried candy, either. For me, it's easy because this is how I grew up. It's harder for people who have tasted this or grew up with candy in the house. I also try not to take any antibiotics or medicine, if possible. Most colds I can cure by eating the right foods or drinking green juice. I believe alcohol, weed, and prescription drugs weaken you. It weakens your ability.

LO: *What would you say is the key to success?*

PV: I believe people are trained to believe they should be happy all the time. That is not life. Life is about happiness *and* struggles, joy *and* pain. Pain is part of life, and we must appreciate both and we must go through both. We must understand that struggling and crisis are where you grow. Growth does not come from the easy times; it comes from the hard times. So when the hard times come, I appreciate them, I learn from them, and they make me stronger. It is not easy. And I don't look for something to numb these feelings; I embrace them. That is why training on the mat is good; we get used to pain. In jiu-jitsu, sometimes we are on the top and sometimes on the bottom. You have to appreciate the bottom as much as the top. When you are on the bottom, you can't quit or take something that is going to make you feel better. Bite your tongue and take it. Learn to appreciate it. I believe in accepting things and dealing with them. I use certain breathing techniques, music, walking on the beach, listening to the ocean, and jumping in the water to cope. Never use artificial things that will only make the situations in your life worse. Deal with what life throws at you naturally.

LO: *What advice would you give someone who feels down or hopeless?*

PV: The secret is sticking with the fundamentals. I believe the way life is designed is, when you do good and surround yourself with good, you attract good into your life. I really believe that. So I think it's the small things. Take care of yourself first. Practice good discipline, nutrition, exercise, sleep, hygiene, and think positively all the time. Focus on being a good person. Be truthful, loyal, respectful; then go out and get it. I don't believe things happen to me; they happen for me, and they happen for a reason. Everything that happens to me is a good thing. I embrace it. So you have to change the narrative. I would say to list all the good things you have in life and move up from there. Embrace your struggles; the worst life to live is a life without struggles.

Pedro Valente is a walking modern-day samurai and has the mind, body, and soul of a sharpened sword. In life, you want the Valente brothers in your corner. To learn more about the Valente brothers, follow them on Facebook, Instagram, YouTube, Twitter, and Periscope @valentebrothers or visit www.valentebrothers.com.

PART ONE

YOU'RE ON YOUR OWN

CHAPTER 1

KNOW THYSELF

"He who makes a beast of himself, gets rid the pain of being man."

DR. SAMUEL JOHNSON

When I graduated college and entered the "real world" at the age of twenty-two, I was lost. I had no outlets to plug into, no rooms to light up, no vision to pursue—I had nothing. There's nothing out there that prepares you for the real world. Unless they pursue a specific career path (doctor, nurse, lawyer, dentist, etc.), most people don't know where they're going in life and what they want, and that's an incredibly debilitating feeling.

I didn't always feel that way, though. In fact, I had a pretty good idea of where my future would take me well before I even reached college. My family ran a business my grandfather started decades ago after he immigrated to the United States. When he was eight, he came via boat with his ten-year-old brother. As a young man, he sold T-shirts, socks, underwear—whatever he could think of—to the Navy men off the piers of New York City. Eventually my grandfather started a company selling uniforms in New York City called Ogulnick Uniforms. My dad and uncle were born into the business and eventually took it over from my grandfather. The company allowed my family to earn a decent living—that is, until New York City stopped recruiting new police officers and my family's main source of income dried up. In those years while New York was on the verge of bankruptcy, I didn't realize that we were barely making it. As a kid, we used our imaginations and played outside until the sun went down. What I did learn, however, was work ethic. Watching my dad head to the office early in the mornings, even on Saturdays, would pay dividends later in my life because I thought hard work was the norm. When I turned thirteen or so, business for my dad began to pick up again. I watched a merger and how to reinvent yourself when things don't go as planned. We were never rich, but my dad was always generous and gave whenever he could. I still remember when my dad said, "If I have the money, I want to give it; but when I don't have it, I can't." I always thought I would follow in my father's footsteps and work at Ogulnick Uniforms, too. *This is what the Ogulnick boys did,* I thought growing up. *This is my future.*

I attended State University of New York at Oneonta even though Ogulnick Uniforms was my destiny—and that mindset may or may not have contributed to my *not* earning a 4.0 GPA. I managed to get decent grades, but I focused more on my fraternity, sports, and having a good time. I had the best of friends, lived the college life to its fullest, and felt as if I was on top of the world. Life was good. And as if it couldn't get any better, after graduation, I backpacked across Europe with one of my best friends for about five weeks on a $1,500 budget. Everything was great, I thought. I had finished college, I was about to have an incredible experience traveling with a good friend, and when I returned home, I would start my career at Ogulnick Uniforms. My future was laid out for me, and I felt secure in the direction I was heading.

Then suddenly without warning, my family decided to sell Ogulnick Uniforms, derailing me from my future. Within one instant, I went from a secure future to zero direction. When I got angry and blamed my father, he said, "Lonnie, in life the hard road ends up the easy one; the easy one ends up the hard one." I looked at him like he was nuts. I wanted the easier one. He didn't know what he was talking about. Or so I thought. Twenty years later and after going through a lot of experiences, I know he was right. There is beauty in the grind and the struggle. You just need to embrace it.

When my family initially sold the business, I was a twenty-two-year-old kid accustomed to being on his own who was now forced to move back in with his parents. Like most Long Island kids, living with my parents was like living with the Costanzas on Seinfeld. They always found something to bicker about. Most Long Island parents are like that, though: married for thirty years, nagging about everything.

"What are you doing with your life?"

"Get a job."

"Are you sending out your résumé?"

Holy shit, was that annoying day in and day out.

And as if things couldn't get any worse, after I moved back into my parents' basement, my girlfriend at the time dumped me, and despite my sending my résumé to endless job openings, not many even acknowledged my application. Unprepared for all of these sudden changes, I was hit with this new reality like a ton of bricks, and it left me in a dark place. I needed to find an outlet to light my way and move out.

“

HE THAT IS GOOD FOR MAKING EXCUSES IS SELDOM GOOD FOR ANYTHING ELSE.

”

BENJAMIN FRANKLIN

I eventually landed my first job at a company called PageNet. The guy who interviewed me also went to my college and was in a rival fraternity. We had a great connection, a great interview, and I was hired. Unfortunately, the job entailed driving through Brooklyn, Queens, and Long Island picking up beepers. It was the worst job, ever. I had interviewed for a sales position, but when the company hired me, they stuck me on deliveries, which was definitely *not* what I wanted to do. I would drop off the beepers and then go home to hang out with friends and play stickball because the job was worthless. I wasn't selling anything. I was just a glorified pager delivery boy.

Let's just say no one was surprised when PageNet fired me a few months later.

One of my fraternity brothers helped me find another job selling local long-distance and Internet cable lines, which were gaining popularity at the time. Notice a theme here? It wouldn't be the first or last time a fraternity brother or college connection helped me throughout my life. To the high school or college kids reading this, practice your relationship-building skills. College offers many clubs, fraternities, sports teams, and so on, so join them all or choose the ones you find interesting. Start building your network from day one. As for my new job, it was a step in the right direction because I was on the phone talking to people and selling. It helped me realize my passion for selling—and that I was good at it. Those around me kept telling me I was a great salesman, but there was one problem: I had no role models in the company, no one to look up to or to offer guidance. It was another dead-end job for me.

Still living in the basement of my parents' home, I started to read anything I could put my hands on to explore my options. I felt lost, and the lack of direction during this period filled me with uncertainty, which caused a lot of pain and suffering.

I read a great book during this time by Tony Robbins. One particular quotation stood out to me, and it has been engrained in my brain ever since: "The whole world loves a winner and has no time for a loser." A spark went off inside me as this quotation hit a cord, and I pondered it for a while. I was done feeling sorry for myself. For my entire youth, I loved sports. I had an insane amount of energy as a boy, and I found an outlet for it by running around any field I could find. Some find their outlet in computers, some in books, and others in music or art. As a kid, for me it was athletics, but I wasn't a kid anymore. I applied to work for the New York Islanders to line my passion for sports with a career, but once again, I never even got a reply. I looked inward to find another outlet—something I'd enjoy, and something that would pave a path to success.

If you're lost and looking for direction, consider listening to those around you. People kept telling me I should be a stockbroker; it was a common theme I kept hearing from those who know me. I loved being around people, I knew that much, and I've always been a people person. Acknowledging that I'm an extrovert and that talking with others came naturally already led me to pursue something in the sales arena. A handful of my friends were in the financial advisory business at the time, and their careers were something I was interested in exploring. After researching, reading, and talking with those in the field, my heart landed on entering the world of finance.

There was one problem, though: In order to become a licensed stockbroker, I had to pass an exam called the Series 7 (also known as the General Securities Representative Exam). I was never a great student, mostly because I didn't think I had to be if would be working at Ogulnick Uniforms. Since I always just got by in school, my head filled with doubt, and I feared I wasn't capable of passing. While my friends partied in the Hamptons, I buckled down to study for the exam. I made a lot of sacrifices during this period because I committed myself to making a change. I was unhappy in my current situation, so I decided to pass on hanging out with friends, partying, and having fun in order to invest in myself and secure my future.

My friend's brother worked at Morgan Stanley during this time and asked me to come in for an interview. Wearing my best suit, I headed in and aced the interview process. All new recruits, however, were also required to pass an academic test. Let's just say I didn't do so well on that part. Morgan Stanley was only hiring experienced brokers, mainly in their mid- to late twenties. They said they liked me and would hire me, but I would have to acquire the appropriate licenses first and get a bit of experience. Excited at the opportunity, I interviewed at several more brokerages in order to get sponsored for the exam. It ended up that my college fraternity brother got me my first job on Wall Street. At that moment, I made a commitment: I was going to pass the Series 7 and become a financial advisor for this firm and then revaluate it after one year.

I compare the sales training program for new recruits at Wall Street firms to be equivalent to the Navy SEALs training program—not from the physical standpoint, of course, but from the attrition rates. At the start of the program, between forty to fifty hopefuls sat with me in class to prepare for and (hopefully) pass the exam. Within just one year, only five to ten people remained. The rigorous nature of passing the Series 7 and starting a business took all of your energy—morning, noon, and night. Anyone who passed the exam and worked for however long on Wall Street gained so many lessons about what it takes to succeed. Even those who left the business ended up becoming successful at whatever they did afterward. This training program was the greatest gift I gave myself—it prepared me for my future and brought me a step closer to achieving my goals. The toughest and most difficult obstacles in life are where the biggest growths happen, especially when you surround yourself with people who operate at a high level and motivate you to keep up. It unleashes a power within you: your beast.

I am proud to say I passed my Series 7, and it was one of the most memorable days of my life. Passing the exam gave me the confidence I needed to bring out something within me that I could not find otherwise. Whether you're taking a test to be a cop, fireman, or accountant, you will feel extreme pride once you pass, and that momentum starts your journey. I didn't think I was capable of passing, but once I overcame my self-doubt, it opened the gateway to endless possibilities. I finally found an outlet to plug into and officially started on my life's mission. Holding a license meant I could work for any company I wanted to, without technically working for them but for myself, since I worked as a contractor, which was incredibly liberating. I loved everything about this career path. I started to research into companies and found ones that were performing well. In 1998, a year after passing my Series 7, I built a business and started getting noticed by senior management. The year after that, there was a bull market and my business started to grow. Some people made comments like, "Oh, you got lucky." What they failed to see was all the pain and work I had to endure for a long period of time in order to build my business and get clients. I wasn't lucky; I don't believe in luck. I believe in hard work and timing. If you work your ass off at something for long enough, good things are bound to happen, but people can call that whatever they want.

This was my first taste of entering beast mode, and I was hooked. Setting goals became a way of life. I wanted to be the best at every aspect of my business. After passing the Series 7 and realizing I was capable of more, I went after other exams. Now mind you, I was a C student my entire life, but once I became passionate, it was easier to focus and apply myself. Don't let your previous academic performance in high school or college hinder you from pursuing new goals. A few years after passing my Series 7, I also passed the Series 63, 24, 9, 10, and 65 and recently earned my real-estate and business brokerage licenses. I passed those exams while working twelve-hour days and studying at night and on weekends. Intelligence is focus and intensity; when you keep your efforts concentrated, you become like a mighty river sweeping all the stands before you. You have to want it.

If you're fortunate enough to find something you're passionate about, something you can plug into, pour every ounce of your soul into it, even if the return on investment isn't all too great in the beginning. I spent a year without making money. I used my contacts and networks to make calls, went out when I didn't want to, and did whatever it took to build my business. I woke up every day ready for battle, with an inner burning desire to make something of myself. Once you achieve one goal, the momentum you've built helps you achieve the next, and the next. I was quickly promoted to managing director, and for the first time in a long time, I finally felt like I was where I was supposed to be.

Knowing thyself is a powerful tool to help guide you through your life. I also learned that some of my personality traits could be harnessed to help me succeed. For example, my dad is from the Bronx and my mom is from Queens, so I've always had a little edge as a child, a little feistiness. You'll find a bit of edginess and feistiness in the majority of beasts. Despite being the skinniest and smallest kid in my grade, in my mind, I was the toughest. As a kid growing up, I often had to defend myself. Despite my small stature, however, fighting wasn't an issue for me because I had quick hands and a fearless attitude. I never looked for fights, weighing seventy pounds (soaking wet), but when you're the littlest kid, you get picked on. My dad taught me never to start a fight but always to defend myself if someone was going to start one with me—so I did. And that's the mind-set I took through life.

When I entered fifth grade, I was shipped off to another school where I only knew a handful of kids. It was a challenging year for me because I had to make a new life for myself. Looking back, though, the experience was beneficial because it put me in an uncomfortable position that forced me to get outside of my comfort zone and make new friends. Whether such experiences directly caused my being a decent salesman today, I don't know. But I do know that when you're put in situations that are terrifying, scary, or uncomfortable, something good will come out of it at some point in your life. It may be one year, five years, or twenty years later, but something good *will* transpire.

I vividly remember one fight I got into in middle school. When the wrestling coach broke us up, he turned to me and said, "You can either go into the principal's office, or you can try out for the wrestling team." He told me I could wrestle kids my size—I was eighty pounds in eighth grade—and that sounded good to me. I tried out, made the wrestling team, and won every match that year. I then became the captain; and later, in high school, I became a two-time all-county wrestler. If I were a true beast, however, I would have put in the extra time and effort into training and have spent my summers honing my skills at wrestling camps in order to increase my chances of becoming the county and state champion. It's something I didn't do, and I regret it. I believe I could have been the state champion, but every beast understands the lessons to be learned in defeat. Those years of training, cutting weight, and waking up early for tournaments planted the seeds for the mind-set I needed in order to succeed in life. When I started as a financial advisor, I related garnering new clients to my experiences as a wrestler—I wanted to get out and win.

LOOK BACK ON YOUR LIFE

Monopoly and poker played a significant role in my childhood; my friends and I would play once a week. By seventh grade, I started collecting, selling, and trading baseball cards, too. I ran a booth selling baseball cards, making markets in Don Mattingly rookie cards and looking for deals on Barry Bonds and Daryl Strawberry mint rookie cards. I would run all the books and find out the card prices, and then I would look for discounts on cards and trade with people in my neighborhood and at card shows. By the age of thirteen, I built a big enough business where I ran my own booth selling cards at Nassau Coliseum and other venues across Long Island. I loved every aspect of the business: strategizing on ways to attract people to my booth, selling, and dealing. My early entrepreneurial spirit extended into ninth grade when I took bets from friends who wanted to wager on any sporting events. I remember the day my dad came into my room, and I told him to open the top desk drawer; it was filled with cash. I told him I had made some sports wagers with some friends, and he shook his head, closed the door, and said, "Just don't tell your mother." I remember spending many weekends mastering the PlayStation game called Wall Street, which I rented from Blockbuster.

Looking back at my childhood and adolescence, I see how my love for Monopoly, my love for poker, and my love for trading baseball cards all correlates to how I discovered my passion for markets and selling. Look back and see what drove and inspired you. This is extremely helpful and insightful for those who are struggling to find an outlet to plug into. Sometimes revisiting your past can help you find your way.

Know your strengths and your weaknesses. I keep a picture on my desk that reminds me of this with a caption that reads, "The United Cerebral Palsy Nassau County Trivia Champions." The picture is of me and three other classmates in seventh grade. One day, my teacher instructed the class to get into groups of four because we were going to compete in a trivia contest against other classes in the school. The winners of my school's trivia contest would travel to the Nassau County championship to represent POB Middle School. My competitive radar immediately went up, and within a few minutes, I grabbed the three smartest kids in my class for my team. We won the school event and went on to win the Long Island championship event. My photo and name were published in the newspaper, and—I can say this with pride—I did not answer a single question during the entire tournament. My gift in this particular situation was identifying the strengths in others. I knew I wasn't the smartest kid, so I circumvented my weakness by teaming up with those who were and therefore could lead us to victory. This is applicable in business and in life. Surround yourself with people who are smarter than you and who are good at what you are not. Build your team recognizing your weaknesses and your strengths.

Building teams, partnerships, and networks is oftentimes more important than trying to do it all by yourself. In today's lone-wolf economy, some of my best partners and greatest ideas came from a podcast, a YouTube video, or an inspirational Facebook post. We'll dive a bit deeper into this in the next chapter, but it is worth noting that we live in a world more interconnected than at any point in history, so the ability to find partners is at your fingertips. Knowing your strengths and weaknesses and then filling in the gaps with whatever resources are available to you will essentially make your strengths even better.

Tapping into your inner beast has nothing to do with altering your being. It's about making the most of the gifts you already have. The key is aligning your innate gifts with your passion. Throw in hard work and determination, and you're on the path to becoming a beast! For example, no matter how hard I try, I will never be a basketball player in the NBA or a quarterback in the NFL. I'll never find success in an environment where size is a prerequisite. That's simply my reality, and I have to accept that and move on. Put me on a sales floor, however, with other salespeople or businessmen, and I will outperform all of them. The passion I have within me allows me to succeed in that environment. Put yourself in an environment where the odds are stacked in your favor. Identify your strengths, and ignite the fire within.

There's great power in knowing who you are in order to help yourself get where you want to be.

INTERVIEW WITH CARYN LUBETSKY

I met Caryn Lubetsky through the community where our kids go to school and where she was always leading a fundraiser for the lower school or volunteering with the running team as a coach. I was always fascinated with her ability as a long-distance runner—probably because the only marathon I ever completed was a triathlon for my color-war team in camp when I was fourteen years old. My interest further peaked when I read about Caryn completing an Ironman while pulling Harvard-educated journalist Kerry Gruson, a quadriplegic, across the finish line (the first female in the world to do that). You can Google Caryn Lubetsky to read more about some of her unbelievable work. I followed Caryn on Facebook as she prepared to run a hundred-mile ultramarathon and said to myself, *I need to interview this woman and find out what goes on in the mind of a mom of three boys, devoted wife, loyal friend, and total beast.*

Let's just say I left this interview high for three days with a desire to become a marathon runner.

LO: *Can you tell me a bit about your childhood and how that plays into who you are today?*

CL: I grew up in New Jersey and was a competitive swimmer from age seven on. I was a six-time state champion in the breaststroke. At fifteen, a bad ski accident ended my competitive swimming career. It was the first time I went to school full-time and realized this whole other world outside of competitive swimming. I left swimming behind me for a while. I tried to make a comeback, but I was not mature enough mentally. As an athlete, your mental state and your mental being is the difference between good and great. It's the difference between competing, enjoying, and thriving, and I was not there at sixteen anymore, so I just began to enjoy my youth. I went to college, law school, got married, and had three kids. I was a lawyer, a wife, a mom, and all the sudden I was turning forty. I had all these roles for other people, but what was I doing for *me*? I went through a bit of a midlife crisis searching for something I can do just for me. My life became about giving and giving, which was incredible, but I needed something for me. I needed something to make me a better wife, mother, and all that. So a month before my fortieth birthday, I decided to run a marathon. I never ran before, and I hated running. Hated it. Living in Miami, the Fort Lauderdale marathon was a week before my birthday, so I decided I was going to run it. I just went out and started running five miles, then ten, fifteen, and then twenty, at which point I felt comfortable enough to run the marathon. I trained for one month, and that was it—I was hooked. I became addicted. I just loved that it was something just for me, and at the same time it was making me a better person in all aspects of my life. I loved the thrill of competition, being back out there, and the thrill of crossing the finish line. I recently turned forty-five, and I have run twenty-five marathons, fifty half marathons, around a thousand 5K's, three full Ironmans, four ultramarathons, and one, hundred-mile marathon.

LO: *What is your favorite book?*

CL: *Born to Run* by Christopher McDougall. It's about how you look at an obstacle, how you overcome an obstacle, and how you deconstruct an obstacle. It teaches you to see what is ahead of you so you can be ahead of it, and how you mentally prepare for these things that seem superhuman or that other people look at and say, "That's impossible." It's really an incredible book and journey.

LO: *How many hours of sleep do you get a night?*

CL: Five to six is my optimal amount. The funny thing is if I sleep more, I am groggy. I set my alarm early so I can get out the door and run. Every couple of weeks I will pass out early and catch up on sleep.

LO: *What do you listen to when you are running?*

CL: I rarely listen to music, and never in a race. I focus on my heart rate, pace, leg turnover, the course, and the competition around me. I am at work; my job is to win!

LO: *Can you tell me what you believe the key to success is?*

CL: I believe it is to lead by example. As a parent, I am showing my children the way to achieve success. Set goals, work hard, and accomplish them. Your body will do whatever your mind tells it. Sports mimics life. Work around the roadblocks. What better way to teach success than to go out and show them how to do it?

LO: *I know you have influenced many people in the Miami area. Can you share a story or two about that?*

CL: I received a phone call from a woman named Sage Kantor who told me following me on Facebook motivated her to make a change in her life. Sage, a mother of two kids and devoted wife, needed a spark. We spoke, and I told her to just start by getting outside and putting one foot in front of the other. That is how it starts. Sage then started running half marathons. Sage transformed her mind and body, shedding fifty pounds. She is a teammate and friend, and I could not be happier for this journey I am on with her. There is a whole world that I am now connected to through the Internet, from Germany to my local teammates who wake up at all hours of the morning and night in order to help train each other for races. This community is like a family, and I believe we all help each other.

LO: *For all the moms out there, what advice would you give them, being a mother of three boys and still finding time to train?*

CL: You need to find balance. For me, that means waking up at 4:30 a.m. I get my hard-core workout in before everyone is up, then I incorporate my kids into my evening workout. The day is much easier taking care of my boys and husband. I sacrifice by getting up early for my family.

LO: *Do you have a day job?*

CL: Yes, I am a professor at Saint Thomas University School of Law, and I teach one class a semester. I am now getting paid by sponsors to run. My main sponsors are Base Performance and On Running, but there's also Chocolate Milk Protein and Carbs who have comped us for events. Local sponsors include Endurance Sports Travel, who sponsored us for an event.

LO: *You recently finished a hundred-mile run. How did you train?*

CL: It came one month after the Boston marathon. I had a coach train me for the Boston marathon, and I took a little time off afterward. I started doing thirty-seven-mile runs, but I don't think I trained that well. The support from my teammates and the huge running community (who are the best people in the world) got me to where I needed to be to finish the race.

LO: *What was it like to experience a hundred-mile run?*

CL: The most incredible experience. It was both the best and the worst. At the high of the day, it was one hundred and fifteen degrees. I had a crew packaging my body with ice; the bottom of my feet were covered in blisters. I just mentally made a decision to enjoy the journey. Whenever it got really tough, I told myself, *I made this decision, so now take a minute to look around and take it in.* I would tell myself that I get to do this, not that I have to. It hurt, and I felt every emotion. I had a crew there to help and encourage me. The last two miles my son ran with me. I felt so lucky we got to have that experience.

LO: *What was the feeling like when you finished the race?*

CL: I started the race at 6:15 a.m. on Saturday and finished at 4:45 a.m. Sunday. It took me twenty-three hours, twenty-eight minutes, and twenty-eight seconds with no stopping for anything except a shoe change at mile fifty. I crossed with my husband, oldest son, and friends. I felt I taught my children to dream big and that you can tackle any obstacle in your way.

LO: *What's the next challenge?*

CL: I am currently recovering from surgery on my foot, but I am looking into Badwater. The next goal will most likely be Badwater.

The Badwater Ultramarathon describes itself as "the world's toughest foot race." It is a 135-mile course starting at 279 feet below sea level in the Badwater Basin, in California's Death Valley, and ending at an elevation of 8,360 feet at Whitney Portal, the trailhead to Mount Whitney. It takes place annually in mid-July when weather conditions can reach temperatures over 120 degrees. Very few people—even among ultramarathoners—are capable of finishing this grueling race.

Caryn is the definition of "heart of a beast." She's an absolute winner and leader because she doesn't make excuses—she makes things happen. Follow her on Facebook (Caryn Vogel Lubetsky) or on Twitter and Instagram @carynlubetsky.

CHAPTER 2

THE LONE-WOLF ECONOMY

"Whoever knocks persistently ends by entering."

ALI, POLITICAL LEADER (AD 600–61)

You have to be a beast right now because you don't have a choice. The economy is changing, and it's making dependency, complacency, and mediocrity increasingly costly. In order to survive in today's economy, you must be proactive. You're in charge of transforming your life into something you want it to be—no one else is. The alternative is to sit idle and wait for things to happen to you (good luck with that). All beasts have a code, and I urge you to adopt it: Create your own destiny.

From 1998 to 2016, we saw Y2K, the boom bust of the tech bubble, a war in Afghanistan, a war in Iraq, a real-estate boom and bust, a collapse of the entire financial system, the War on Terror, QE1, 2, and 3, nuclear implosion in Japan, Operation Twist, and United Kingdom leaving the European Union. We live in a world of rolling bubbles and constant change, all of which are out of our personal control. Global interest rates have never been lower, and experiments never before tried are being made—all in an attempt to prop up the economy. The end result is uncertain, and in many cases, it causes fear. In order to survive, you have to adapt and figure out how to get up, move forward, and continue on your personal path to success. We live in a world increasingly dominated by government intervention, so if you're going to be an entrepreneur, you have no choice but to become a beast.

In January 2016, the S&P 500 had its worst start of the year, ever. Regardless of what business you're in, the stock market tends to be a leading indicator for the rest of the economy. Generally speaking, if the stock market drops pretty hard, the real-estate market follows, then the rest of the economy suffers. When the stock markets do well, people feel wealthier and tend to spend more, and the economy grows. The stock market is known as a leading indicator for the economy. There are currency wars between the United States, China, and other governments;

and oil—as of the writing of this book—is in its own bursting of a bubble. It's difficult to predict what the final outcome will be. After the 2008 crisis, the term "black swan" entered the lexicon, meaning black swan events are impossible to predict yet have catastrophic ramifications. No one ever or rarely sees a black swan, but they are out there. What we are witnessing these days is an experiment with financial engineering by federal governments around the world. Looking at the markets over time and history, these types of events are often considered crises. But when we look back now, they were merely blips on the radar. The crash of 1987 was devastating to investors in many markets, but it's barely talked about today. Long-term strategies and diversification offer the best defense to many of these short-term setbacks.

What are our choices in a world filled with such uncertainty? Is there such a thing as job security? If you have a job, you have to look over your shoulder at all times because someone may look to replace you or fire you. Corporations are ruthless in attaining their bottom line, and if your company is struggling and not bringing in revenue, it will usually start fixing its revenue problem by cutting employees. I have watched this happen to friends and family members one too many times with devastating results. If hardships like these happen to us, we often look for people to blame, but we can't, because that's a short-term fix that does not help. Instead, you need to find the tools necessary to get motivated and change your life for the better.

THE HEART OF A BEAST = VISION + PREPARATION + PERSISTENCE + PATIENCE

It's up to you to survive in today's lone-wolf economy; you must find the answers, tactics, and strategies to carry your business forward. It is therefore helpful to find a career path you enjoy waking up to. Once you're passionate about what you're doing, you're more likely to do it well and unlock the beast living within you. It helps a great deal to like what you are doing because when things get tough and your brain fills with thoughts of quitting, you'll have your passion to fall back on, and that will keep you going.

The three most important keys are preparation, persistence, and patience. First, you have to create that vision we covered in the introduction. Once you have your vision, it's time to roll up your sleeves and work. If your vision is to be an Olympic gold medalist in wrestling, preparation means studying every match you can get your hands on, reading about previous champions, listening to interviews about your competition, studying the strategies of Dan Gable (the greatest wrestler of all time), and so on. Understanding every insight and trick maneuver could give you an edge in each match you're going to face. Preparation is doing everything in your power to get yourself ready.

Buffet underperformed the S&P 500 by between 20 and 40 percent in a given year, which is hard to believe considering the long-term returns he has put up. No strategy will work all the time on a year-over-year basis; that is very difficult to do. Patience has helped him earn his fortune. I don't know many millionaires who acquired their wealth overnight.

If you're patient, and you work through the inevitable obstacles, any success you achieve will be the result of your preparation, your persistence, and your patience—and with that you'll be much better able to handle any arrows, rocks, and problems thrown at you as well.

CREATING PARTNERSHIPS

The beauty of becoming a beast is you'll attract other beasts into your life; positive energy is contagious. That is the good part; the bad part is that you also need to be wary of those who might be drawn to you and wish to partner with you. Partnerships can be difficult because people have unequal work ethics. If there is not a clear, defined job description for each person in the partnership, the odds of failure increase. For example, take two cops walking the beat writing tickets in New York City. One reads the license plate number, the other writes the ticket. That partnership works because each person has a specific role. Be sure to evaluate the pros and cons before entering any sort of partnership—business or personal. Oftentimes, it is easier to get in than it is to get out.

This doesn't mean all partnerships are bad, but it's important to have each person's roles clearly defined. I personally have a partnership with several people and entities. My firm's asset-allocation division runs my clients' assets, and we have a great partnership. They provide a service I pay for, and we thus have a clearly defined relationship. Your accountants, your attorney, your therapist, your instructors—these are partnerships. Anyone you exchange money with is basically a partner. Even close friends, to some degree, are partners.

We have partnerships with people who are our mentors. These partnerships may not be face-to-face, nor do you necessarily need to have a close relationship with all of your mentors, but mentors will influence certain business decisions you make. For example, I subscribe to newsletters, listen to podcasts all the time, and watch YouTube videos from people who can provide me with enormous amounts of valuable information. Even though I might not have met these people, I find value in what they're putting out in the world and therefore view them as partners. Our world of interconnectivity today allows us access to more people than ever before. On the same token, it's important for you also to do your research. In this world of infinite access, there are a lot of ways to waste your time. Make sure these partners are worth your while and that they're going to add value to your life. I always go to bed with a book in my hand or an earpiece in my ear. What you're getting out of the experience should be leading you toward a positive path that'll give you fuel for the next day. Oftentimes the greatest fuel in the world is music; it is therapeutic on so many levels. Whether you are in the gym on your last set and your favorite Metallica song comes on, or you are in the car jamming to some old-school Run-D.M.C., it doesn't matter. The point is to fire up your favorite tunes whenever possible.

Don't do business or engage in a partnership with those who only have eyes for themselves and their bank accounts. Do business with good people whose goals are to enhance other people's lives. I can't stress this enough. Always look at the heart of the person. It is the most important character trait in any human being. The money will follow.

Early in my career, I came up with a formula for success: Relationships plus salesmanship equals business. Within that relationship, the single most important component is trust. You have to create relationships regardless of the business you're in, and building quality relationships takes time and effort. Every business needs clients to service, so relationships are key. It doesn't cost money to be nice or friendly, or to go out of your way to help another person, whether that's a friend, client, or partner. When you do that, you gain trust, confidence, and—the most important currency of all—human capital.

Once you are solely focused on the other person's needs, and not your own, success follows like the night follows day. In my line of work, I feel as if I have to be a CIA agent or Sherlock Holmes combined with Sigmund Freud. Financial advisors, like all entrepreneurs, have to be good at the art of intelligence gathering and be versed in human psychology. In other words, know your customer. If you can't identify the needs of the people you're doing business with and you don't understand who your clients are, you're going to be at a major disadvantage. You can practice gathering social intelligence and studying human psychology by being active or reading books. Start by finding events that interest you, networking, talking to other people, and asking questions to those who can teach you what your market values and what it doesn't value. You can research it through books, audiobooks, or the Internet, where all the information you need is directly at your fingertips. Subscribe to Audible.com to listen to audiobooks if you don't want to read. I love to read and highlight books, but with a wife and two kids, time is hard to come by, so I listen to audiobooks in the car or on dog walks—these are the best times for me to pick up more knowledge. Mowing the lawn, bike riding, and running are all great times to plug in to your favorite podcast or audiobook. Do it, and you will be smarter tomorrow.

Many times in the lone-wolf economy, there will be a

“

EVERY STRIKE BRINGS ME CLOSER TO THE NEXT HOME RUN.

”

BABE RUTH

need to form or join a team. Each team needs to establish a leader who makes all the decisions, and when possible, that leader should be you. Too many chefs in the kitchen is never a good thing and leads to confusion, chaos, and arguments. You should form a team to accomplish a goal where each member has a specific job that's unique to his skill set—that's when a team can do great things. Depending on your goals, you'll likely reach a point where you're going to want to build a team since you're not going to be able to do everything by yourself anyway. If one man is a salesman, another man is an analyst, the third is a trader, and the fourth is an operations guy. If everybody plays well in his or her position, then your team is on the path to accomplishing great things.

The outer layer of your team consists of your allies—people who over time have formed bonds and relationships with you. You look out for them, and they look after you. You may not be partners, per se, but when they come across someone who is in need of a specific service in your field, they are going to immediately refer that person to you. Word-of-mouth references are a result of the partnerships and relationships you've established throughout your business journey.

YOU ARE NOT ALONE

The lone-wolf economy sounds like you're alone, but technically you're not. It *does* mean that, as a human being who wants to survive and grow, you have to rely on yourself, but you can learn from others without depending on others. Social media has become a lion's den for future entrepreneurs and beasts who are taking business to a whole new level because the opportunities to connect are exponential. Work to build a huge Rolodex, grow your Facebook following, grow your connections on LinkedIn, follow people on Twitter, or grow your network through Snapchat and Instagram stories. Don't be scared to post; be yourself and be bold. People will respect you. Forget those who make fun or talk shit; they have their own issues, and it's none of your business. Social media tools can only help you. If you've recently met someone, send him a request on LinkedIn, follow her on Twitter, invite them to like your Facebook business account. You never know when social media connections can grow into a prosperous entrepreneurial business where millions of dollars can be made.

Social media forums also offer a way for people—especially new clients or prospects—to get to know you. I use social media because it's a way for people to learn about me, my family, and the type of person I am. I also think it's pretty cool that several generations down my family tree will be able to know me, my family, and my friends. I would love to click online and check how the Ogulnicks lived and what they were like five generations ago.

Having a positive social media presence is a good way of gaining confidence and trust in your prospective business relationships. Also, you'd be surprised at how many people you can convert into clients by simply connecting with them. It's an unbelievable way for friends, clients, and prospects to keep in touch. Maybe you haven't spoken to somebody in fifteen years and you wish him or her a happy birthday. This leads to exchanging some more back-and-forth messages, and you both reconnect, and a spark ignites. Before you know it, you're in business together. Staying in touch with people provides opportunities with the greatest payback for the least amount of effort; you should not dismiss these opportunities.

I've seen this happen, and in fact, it happened to me recently. An absolute beast in my business reached out to me—someone whom I don't personally know, but we are connected on LinkedIn. Don sent me a congratulations text message through the LinkedIn application just as I was reading his new book on financial advisory practices. We exchanged a few messages back and forth, and before I knew it, I was speaking with his team about the best advisory coaching program in the business. I'd been thinking about using Don's coaching platform for a few years, and with a simple LinkedIn congratulations notification, he converted an online connection into a client. It was a win-win situation where Don acquired new business and I acquired knowledge to grow a stronger practice.

Whatever level of beasthood you think you're at, there are ten levels above you, and then ten levels above that. You always have more to learn and more knowledge to gain; self-improvement never ends, and it never will, because the game is constantly changing.

INTERVIEW WITH EMIL PALDINO

Born in France and growing up in Sweden, this low-key fitness guru has built a business and a following the old-school way. Never once having a business card, he was the Bryan brothers' fitness trainer—perhaps the greatest doubles team to ever hit tennis courts—as well as the trainer for countless other professionals and models. Getting even a half-hour appointment with Emil is nearly impossible. After rehabilitating my shoulder injury through weight training, the only rehabilitation method I was aware of, one of my best friends explained to me that I needed a total-body workout combining strength training and cardio. He recommended Emil, but his only available time slot was 6:00 a.m., which he opened up specifically for me. I was in! Emil is a beast—a true, old-school man's man who lives with a code of ethics and discipline that is contagious. You don't want to show up at 6:01 a.m., either. Although he's a gentle giant and someone I am happy to consider a friend, Emil is not the type of guy you want to piss off.

LO: *What is your athletic background?*

EP: My father was a professional boxer, so he taught me how to fight. Since I was eight years old, I played high-level sports, all different sports, ultimately playing semi-pro soccer. My brother was a fourth-degree black belt in Tae Kwon Do. I, too, started in Tae Kwon Do and ended up as a black belt in Walu Kung Fu, which is a more efficient style of Kung Fu martial arts that requires more discipline. In essence, Walu Kung Fu is the art of breaking bones, which taught me confidence and calmness.

LO: *How did you get into personal training?*

EP: When I came out of college, there were no jobs, but I had to find a job to make a living. In Europe, I decided to get into training by taking all my skills from sports and teaching them to others. Once I started, there was no turning back. My love for helping people combined with my hobby turned into my job. I am now a qualified corrective-exercise specialist, a performance-enhancement specialist, and a personal-trainer specialist. I am currently studying to coach as an MMA specialist. I'm studying diets, fitness, moves, and new techniques every day.

LO: *How did you build your business?*

EP: I started running a spa where I met and worked with a lot of people. I loved the profession, and people could sense that. I always believed I had so much to offer. My code of ethics is to be very professional, educated—100 percent on time—and always honest. I eventually went off on my own, and through word of mouth, my businesses grew.

LO: *How did you end up training the Bryan brothers?*

EP: For thirteen years, it was strictly word of mouth. I've never made a business card. My base clients stay with me and spread the word.

LO: *What is the secret for that loyalty with all the competition today?*

EP: For me, I don't just do the job to make money. I love my job, I love challenges, and I love when someone comes to me and needs my help. I know I have so much to offer my clients. I think the key is to be passionate about helping people.

LO: *What is your favorite book?*

EP: *Candide* by Voltaire and anything by Shakespeare.

LO: *How many hours of sleep do you get?*

EM: Six hours at night with a half-hour nap midday. It gives me more energy for the second half of the day.

LO: *Do you drink alcohol?*

EP: Not anymore. When I was young, I had fun, but I quit cold turkey six years ago. I got sick with pneumonia, and I stopped drinking after that. The first year of not drinking was a transition, but after that it was easy. I have zero interest in alcohol because it is very bad for your health. I prefer grape seeds in the morning; they're healthier than wine.

LO: *What do you need to work on?*

EP: I'm always looking for ways to be a better person.

LO: *How often do you work out?*

EP: Six to seven times per week for forty-five minutes to an hour and a half, and tennis once a week.

LO: *What's your favorite exercise?*

EP: Pull-ups, twenty to thirty without stopping.

LO: *Any advice or words of wisdom for someone looking to get out of a rut?*

EP: It can always be worse. As long as you are breathing, there is hope. Start exercising so you feel better, and that will open doors for you.

LO: *What technique do you use to prevent you from losing your temper?*

EP: Take five very deep breathes. They should last a couple of minutes, so that should be enough time for you to cool down.

In an era of social media dominance, there are time-tested principles that last thousands of years—honesty, punctuality, passion, discipline, hard work, leading by example, and friendship. When you have these qualities, your business will grow through your brand. And your brand is what others say about you when you're not around. Emil is an absolute, total beast!

CHAPTER 3

YOUR HEALTH

"Early to bed, early to rise makes a man healthy, wealthy, and wise."

BENJAMIN FRANKLIN

Taking care of your body and getting physically stronger, faster, and better is an essential step in entering beast mode and maximizing your full potential. It's not just the physical aspect of being healthy that is important; the mental aspect is important, too. If your mind-set is off and if you're not in a good place, then you can't be a good husband, a good wife, a good father, a good friend, a good employee, a good advisor, and so on. You can't be good at anything if you're not good in the mind. Taking care of your body and mind is a crucial component, and every beast will tell you doing so is one of the greatest keys to success.

In the previous chapter, we went over how the world is interconnected economically and how downturns affect businesses locally, nationally, and globally. Regardless of your career, business, or if you're a stay-at-home parent, global economic actions eventually trickle down and affect us all. We have to focus on what we *can* control: the decisions we make while things happen around us. We have the personal responsibility, therefore, to start our day in a good state of mind. By doing so, you will better handle any unexpected challenges throughout the day; by not doing so, things can unravel, and you will likely make the situation worse.

You start your day mentally strong by exercising.

The by-product of being disciplined and working hard in business is money in your bank account. Similarly, the by-product of getting your mind right with exercise is becoming physically fit. Working out is just as much a mental exercise as it is a physical one. A person with a good physique also has a strong mind who is immensely dedicated and committed to his goals. He also made a lot of sacrifices to get there. If you're hitting the gym consistently and with intensity, you're committing both mentally and physically to your goal.

I recommend working out in the morning. Set the tone for

the day by focusing your energy and putting everything you have into your morning workout. When you complete a high-intensity workout, you'll get a little buzz; exercising releases endorphins in the brain and makes you feel great afterward. We live in a culture where the vast majority of people view working out as a chore—and it shouldn't be that way. We should *reward* our bodies with exercise—and we should want to do it. If our bodies could speak, they would whine, complain, and beg us for movement. Make it a priority to gift those endorphins to your body because your mind will also reap the benefits. When you start your day strong with pushing yourself through a challenging workout, those endorphins will spill over to the rest of your day when you're engaging with your clients, making a sales presentation, or finishing up the latest project for your boss. Your mind-set will be in a sharper state, and you'll be able to deal with stress more easily.

The term *beast* and the phrase "beast mode" are echoed all over gyms across the world. Go to any gym in the country, and you will see beasts littered all around, crushing workouts with everything they have. The majority of these people consider the gym their therapist, myself included. The gym—and more broadly speaking, working out and being physically active—is what we do to get our minds right. It then becomes an addiction.

Most of us are aware of the negative effects of not working out. Those who don't work out oftentimes feel sluggish. People are less focused on days they don't work out. As we age, those who don't take care of their minds and bodies find themselves slipping as their work gets more demanding. There is a long list of medical reasons to be active: hypertension, diabetes, heart failure, but there are also a lot of mental illnesses that are caused by inactivity, too. In a 2013 study published in the *American Journal of Preventive Medicine*, researchers reviewed thirty large studies on depression and found that twenty-five of those studies confirmed that people who don't exercise have a higher risk of depression. In addition, if you don't exercise, you may be missing out on the preventative and potentially healing effects on a wide range of mood disorders. The good news is that even if you're obese, unhealthy, or depressed, you can fix it. There are four basic components to taking care of yourself.

GOD'S "LITTLE BLUE PILL": SLEEP

The first component is sleep. We've all heard that adults should get at least eight hours of sleep every night, and for good reason: Sleeping is vital. I call a good seven to eight hours of sleep God's "little blue pill"—it truly does wonders. If I wake up without seven or eight hours' worth of sleep, I am a different human being. Lack of sleep makes me irritable and, at times, completely unproductive. There are some people who claim they can operate on three, four, or five hours of sleep, but they are a rare breed and an exception to the rule. There's no way in hell I can operate at my peak running on four or five hours of sleep—it just won't happen.

Prioritizing my sleep and starting each day with a workout changed my life. It also helped me weather some of the harsh storms the economy has surprised us with in the last few years. I can't even imagine tackling life's day-to-day problems without having a good night's sleep. A little trick many beasts employ is a quick ten- to twenty-minute catnap in the late afternoon. If you're tired or sluggish after lunch, lie down on the floor, put your legs up on a chair to get the blood flowing, and close your eyes for ten to twenty minutes. Even if you don't fall asleep, set your phone or Fitbit for twenty minutes and tune everything out. After the twenty minutes are up, get up and tackle the second half of your day, fresh. This can do wonders for your productivity.

If you suffer from restless nights, insomnia, or general bad sleeping patterns, do yourself a favor: Do some research, study, read books, and if necessary, go see a sleeping specialist—you need to address it. There are professionals who can help you. I challenge you to commit to sleeping seven to eight hours every night for a month and to track your changes mentally, emotionally, and physically. I promise it will blow you away.

NUTRITION

The second key component to taking care of yourself is eating right. A few years ago, I noticed a friend of mine eating healthy and working out every morning. I asked him randomly what he ate for breakfast, and he told me he blends frozen fruits (such as bananas, strawberries, and mangos) with pomegranate, orange juice, coconut water, and flax seeds. Since that day a couple of years ago, I have adopted that breakfast.

During a visit to Boca Raton, I decided to stop into a juice bar called Raw Juce (@RawJuce) and hang with my buddy Barry, aka Brap. We got to talking over a cacao protein crunch acai bowl, which was absolutely delicious. While conversing, I inquired about what got him into the health business. This is what he said:

"In January 2009, I noticed a large lump in my throat, which unfortunately turned out to be cancer. My surgery took place in March 2009, and for the following year, I just wasn't feeling myself; I was tired and depressed. I didn't have any motivation, which was the exact opposite of how I was my whole life. I was always full of high energy and positivity, wanting to conquer the world—and now I had trouble getting out of my house some days. I looked for ways to feel better and stumbled upon juicing. From the very first glass, I felt better. My energy came back, my passion came back, my mind got clearer, my skin got tighter—it was amazing. I started telling everybody around me what juicing was doing for me, so much so that I finally said I've got to do something with this, maybe open a juice bar. I didn't have any expertise in a "fast casual" business [*places like Starbucks and Chipotle are called fast casual*], so I approached my friend/neighbor, who had some experience in retail, and told him we needed to open a juice bar. He noticed my body was better physically, changing from juicing all day and working out like crazy. He did his due diligence and researched the power of juicing and liked what he saw. We then started working on the concept of Raw Juce, and here we are."

To learn more about the benefits to juicing, Brap recommended reading *How Not to Die* by Dr. Michael Greger, MD. According to Dr. Greger, if a plant-based diet (eating fruits, vegetables, nuts) were a drug, it would be the best drug in the world, as it cures everything. There is scientific data on how it helps people with diabetes, cholesterol, skin problems—the whole gambit. When you get rid of the processed foods, along with processed meat, your body explodes with energy. Between the steroids, antibiotics, and chemicals injected into all the meat commercially produced, we don't really know what we are consuming. Dr. Greger's book is informative from a statistical standpoint on how to eat healthy.

There is so much packaged and processed garbage out there marketed for us to consume, not to mention the millions of different diets claiming to be the answer to your problems. A complete beast will take his nutrition to the max and eat cleanly all day long, but on a realistic level, what you should focus on is finding what works for you.

The diet I've created that works for me is called the energy diet. I made it up. If something is going to take away from my energy level, I won't eat it. It's a simple formula I apply from the moment I wake up in the morning to the moment I go to bed at night. Come Saturday night, though, I break all rules and reward myself with whatever I want. My diet isn't perfect, but it doesn't have to be perfect. A beast doesn't necessarily strive for perfection; he strives for excellence. Everything is fine for us as long as it's in moderation, but you better be conscious of what you're putting in your body and focus on what works for you. There's a variety of different ways to eat today, but if you want to perform at your highest level of potential, then that McDonald's Big Mac and French fries for lunch every week isn't the best idea. Use Google to learn about the array of diets that may help you. I am currently reading the Gracie diet, picking up pointers from Rorion Gracie, the son of Hélio Gracie, and listening to Dr. Greger's book, *How Not to Die*, in my car while driving to work.

"

PHYSICAL FITNESS IS NOT ONLY ONE OF THE MOST IMPORTANT KEYS TO A HEALTHY BODY, IT IS THE BASIS OF DYNAMIC AND CREATIVE INTELLECTUAL ABILITY.

"

JOHN F. KENNEDY

AVOIDING ALCOHOL

At the beginning of the year in January, while flipping through my Instagram feed, a thirty-day no-alcohol challenge popped up from Australian-American investor and TV and podcast host James Swanwick. His post encouraged his followers to take the challenge in order to improve their lives. He himself stopped drinking after being a party animal. After the first thirty days, he lost thirteen pounds, had more money in his bank, slept better, and was more productive, among other improvements. He felt so amazing after his first thirty days that he decided to continue not drinking and hasn't since 2010. In that Instagram post, he wrote, "Feel better, look better, lose weight, save money, and have better relationships." At forty years old, I decided to take the challenge. At that time, it had been over twenty years since I went more than thirty days without a sip of alcohol. To the surprise of many of my friends—and even myself—I completed the thirty-day challenge and yielded some amazing results myself. Feeling good (and proud), I decided to continue the challenge. Thirty days turned into sixty, and sixty turned into ninety. I can happily say today that the days of waking up with a hangover are long gone.

There are several studies out there that claim a glass of wine every night is good for you. Whether that's true or not is hard to confirm since five scientists will give you five different answers. When it comes to alcohol, just like nutrition, you have to find what works for you. If a glass every night works for you, that's great. Personally, I find that one glass of wine or a couple of cocktails severely disrupts my sleep and then negatively affects my morning. If something is hurting me instead of helping me, I don't do it. It is as simple as that. The general rule is if you don't feel good the next day, then don't do it—and that goes for anything. The amount of alcohol intake is a personal decision only you can make because only you know how it's going to affect you.

EXERCISE

The fourth component is exercise. Becoming faster, stronger, and better on a daily basis is the final component to achieving your maximum potential. The habit of pushing yourself outside of your comfort zone and never giving up is the greatest gift you can give yourself.

I grew up athletic, so exercising has always been a natural part of my life, but I didn't really start pushing myself until my wrestling in high school. My natural ability in wrestling only took me to a certain level. I worked hard, but the county and state champions worked harder; they were animals. Beasts go above and beyond what is normal; it's their grit, toughness, and sacrifices that allow them to rise to the top. Those guys went above and beyond what I was willing to do at that time in my life, and it showed.

I didn't earn the title of champion because I didn't put in enough work and, instead, came in third place. You know what the champion did over the summer? He sacrificed his summer to attend an elite wresting academy in Iowa. You know what I did? I went camping with my friends—that's the difference. He wasn't more talented than I was, per se (I beat him the year before), but he just put in more time and effort. Your level of success depends on your commitment and how much further you are willing to work. I remembered that lesson, and from then on, I started putting in more effort into everything that I did.

There is, however, a small nugget of positivity that came out of this experience. Although I lost one match and wanted to quit, I couldn't. I needed to win my next four matches in order to take third place in Nassau County. I channeled my anger and shredded through them like a beast and held my head high on the podium. I look back at that time, and although I didn't place first in the county tournament, I persevered through a setback and attained a worthy goal.

In wrestling, cutting weight is what wrestlers do in order to compete in the weight class that will give them the most optimal advantage. Ideally, you want to be the biggest and the strongest in your weight class, so in order for me to have competed in my optimal weight class for the next tournament, I had to lose twenty pounds. I was determined to do it. Sucking on orange-juice ices and eating lettuce dinners may not have been the healthiest of choices, but I was able to lose the weight, compete, and win. I became a two-time all-county wrestler. Looking back at it now, it was the first time I set goals for myself, even though I didn't realize I was doing so at the time. It was a great lesson in discipline and hard work.

I also played soccer during high school. As a junior, I wanted to start on the varsity soccer team, but I fell ill with mononucleosis during "hell week" of tryouts. I didn't let my sickness come in the way of my goal, though. I had to make my mark on the team, so despite feeling weak, I attended each day of soccer practice. After practice one day, the coach instructed each team member to run his fastest mile. I ran the mile as fast as I could, and at the end of the race, I passed out on the field and needed to be carried off. I might have pushed myself too far, but come hell or high water, I was starting on that team. That's what beasts do; they put in everything they have. There are no sick days. Not only did I make the varsity team, but I ended up being an all-conference soccer player.

The bonds you make on the sports field last a lifetime. Your teammates when you're growing up stay your teammates for life. The combo of wrestling (an individual sport) and soccer (a team sport) gave me great life skills that I use every day. As a father of two young girls, I hope that my kids will also be exposed to both individual and team sports because the value in them is so powerful.

At an early age, I learned and developed skills for being a winner. Fast-forward to today, and waking up at 5:15 in the morning to go to the gym is normal for me. It's not easy, but I have to do it. My experiences as an adolescent lead me to the habit of working out and pushing myself to my maximum potential.

STARTING OUT

If you didn't grow up athletic as a child, or if you don't have the natural desire to work out because it wasn't really instilled in you as a young person, you're not alone. The best thing for those new to working out or being active is to find a group. This group can range from a gym membership or a yoga studio to the craze with CrossFit and boot-camp gyms. If you need a little motivation, watch *Fittest on Earth* on Netflix—it's about the Reebok CrossFit games. Those people are absolute beasts—mind and body—and you can tell that they love what they do. You might not be someone who wants to lift weights. Or you might hate running. Or you might hate the gym. That's okay. There are a lot of ways to move your body. If you're just starting out, take a half-hour walk around the block when you wake up. Or check out the hundreds of at-home DVD programs. There's also biking, hiking, and swimming. Try everything until you find something you enjoy and that works for you. Then find thirty to sixty minutes—preferably in the morning—to put in the work every day.

Be realistic with your goals, especially in the beginning. If you've never run before, don't expect to start running a 5K in a week; it takes time. Be patient with yourself, and do what you can. Your daily four-mile walk in the morning can slowly turn into a jog. Before you know it, you'll be jogging the entire four miles, and then you can start pushing yourself and picking up the pace. You might find a local running group to join and start a training program. Soon after that, you'll be doing a half marathon, then a full marathon.

Developing a new habit of working out won't be easy, either. The first few days are the hardest, but you have to push through and force yourself out the door. You might not like it or want to do it, but you have to get over it because your mind and body need it.

If you struggle getting going in the morning, try jumping in the shower when you first wake up. I read in a health journal that doing so is equal to thirty minutes more of sleep. Play with the hot and cold water to get the blood really circulating. It's a little trick I've adopted that helps me get out the door with greater ease, especially since it wakes me up and I don't feel groggy or tired afterward.

Once you exercise for a month, it will become a habit. Working out changes your life for the better, as long as you're putting in the work and effort.

MIXING IT UP

After a while—and you will know when—you'll want to change your routine, not just for the physical benefits, but because it also keeps you from getting stuck in a rut. You'll want to change your routine up because your body will be able to do more—it's a natural progression. Changing your workout every few months keeps things fresh, interesting, and new.

I was forced to mix up my workout routine after I sustained a shoulder injury. A physician told me either I would need surgery or I could build the muscle around the injury. I chose the latter and spent about a year rehabilitating my shoulder by aggressively lifting weights. It gave me the spark I needed at the time to switch things up, get back to the gym, and start lifting again since I wasn't doing much besides tennis. The physical gains and the increase in strength from changing my routine changed my body and my confidence—it made me feel great.

Unfortunately, playing tennis for ten years also left me with a really bad elbow injury that recently cut down my tennis hours significantly. I changed my routine yet again due to that injury and started taking core boot-camp cardio classes—thirty to sixty minutes of hell. The level of intensity is up to each individual. If you choose to cut corners, you're only cheating yourself. With my weekly tennis games over, I began my journey as a white belt in Brazilian jiu-jitsu, which was an exciting new challenge for me. Getting back on the mats for me was like going back to high school.

Whether you've sustained an injury, plateaued, or are simply bored, changing your workout routine is beneficial. If you get injured, don't give up or stop working out; there's always something else you can work on.

Do something every day that sucks in the moment. The rewards you get will be ten times the pain you went through, I promise. A fundamental quality of being a beast is always challenging yourself—embrace challenges and don't be scared of being a beginner; we all have to start somewhere. There's a saying in jiu-jitsu: "A black belt is a white belt who did not quit."

One of the best strategies for getting started and keeping the momentum is envisioning you are someone you admire. It's a bit of a mind trick you can play on yourself, and I do this all the time with all aspects of my life. When I walk to the gym, I find a video on YouTube of my workout for that day. I find the biggest beast, watch his video, and then copy his workout. If I am going to the gym to lift heavy, I watch a man named Ulisses—the guy is a monster. By the time I make it to the gym and begin working out, in my mind I, too, am that beast. When I work out with that mentality, I naturally get bigger and stronger. If I'm going to play tennis, I watch Novak Djokovic before my match, and I study his movements on my walk to the tennis court. When I go to jiu-jitsu, I watch Valente Brothers jiu-jitsu videos or Kron Gracie matches. When I go to the office, I listen to podcasts pertaining to my business to get my mind prepared for the day. You get my point. Use every minute to study and get better at what you're doing. Fill your brain with the best people in the world.

You're not reinventing the wheel; you're looking for inspiration from others who are succeeding in the way you want to succeed. You want to tap into what their mentality is like because if they're successful in a certain aspect, then you want to know how they got there. With all the social media platforms at your fingertips, you really have no excuse not to be inspired. There's not a day that goes by that I'm not on YouTube watching and learning, or listening to a podcast to soak up as much knowledge and information as I possibly can. Knowledge is power. The beauty of all of this is that it's free, so take advantage of it. Google can answer almost any question to any problem you might have.

It's important to give yourself time away from the stress and pressures of life, too. Don't be afraid to push yourself a little bit to get out on the mountain and find an adventure. I have no problem taking on a new challenge, and neither should you. Nothing in the world makes me happier than shredding down a mountain full of fresh powder, taking a Jet Ski ride, exploring a new bike trail, or taking a nice walk to decompress. Outdoor adventures offer the opportunity to tune the world out for a few brief moments in which you can really enjoy life. Whatever it is you love to do, find the time to do it. You will recharge your batteries and come back fully lit with energy, drawing people toward you.

LIKE ATTRACTS LIKE

If you go to the gym every morning at 6:30, it puts you in contact with like-minded people. Any time you walk into a gym, you're immediately surrounded by beasts. Beasts love other beasts because they feed off each other. These people are pushing themselves to be better. The gym is where friendships and relationships are formed—and from that, opportunities. The longer you practice whatever activity you choose, the more easily you will make new friends who will change your life for the better. Do things you love to do, and you will find others just like you.

At this point in the book, we've covered a large portion of getting yourself on track—who you are and what you can do to improve yourself. Getting your mind and body on track sets the tone for your journey to becoming a beast. Now we'll be transitioning into the action phase. Developing skills that help establish and maintain relationships is a key component of becoming a beast. For some people, these skills come naturally—public speaking, working with big groups, one-on-one negotiations. For others, these are painstaking operations. For the latter, you're in luck; there are secrets and strategies. For the former, this is the time to sharpen the sword.

INTERVIEW WITH SAMANTHA CHRISTINA SANCHEZ

Known as @littlebeastss on Instagram, Samantha Sanchez is a sought-after Personal Fitness Instructor at Barry's Bootcamp in Miami. One of my best friends and workout partners asked me one day if I wanted to try a boot-camp class one morning. At this point, I had been consistently working out every day at 6:00 a.m., feeling good and up for any and all challenges, so obviously I said yes. I walked into this boot-camp class and found music blasting and a five-foot ball of energy spitting out her quotation of the day and reviewing the hour of hell we were about to endure. Right away, I saw that she brought out the best in everyone around her, and for that reason, I needed to know more about this "little beast."

LO: *How did you get into working out?*

SS: I was in gymnastics and competitive cheerleading, which I did for about ten years each. In the middle of high school, my cheerleading became really expensive with all the travel. Being one of five kids, I had to stop doing competitive cheerleading. In 2007, at the age of sixteen, I began to notice my mood changes and weight gain and realized quickly that I needed to exercise. I researched online, looked up workouts, and started creating some in my garage. I started to look and feel good again. I started working, which allowed me to afford gym memberships, and I worked out seven days a week—spinning, Pilates, everything. I realized no matter what was happening in my life, I would find time to work out. It was a passion of mine. While attending the University of Florida in Gainesville, I was still writing up workouts, training friends and roommates. They thought I was crazy. Toward the end of college, I was able to experiment with outdoor boot camps in Miami, leading more than forty people in a park—it was awesome. I then ran marathons for a couple of years. I wanted to up the intensity, so I found CrossFit, fell in love, and went full force into that. I felt my competitive juices flowing again. I would get recruited for teams. I met the owners of The Fit Shop NMB through the CrossFit industry, and that's how I became part of The Fit Shop NMB family.

LO: *Where did #littlebeast come from?*

SS: Being five feet tall and winning competitive mud runs, I started being called "little beast" by everyone, so the name stuck and became sort of my brand now.

LO: *What do you think a beast is?*

SS: People who are relentless in pursuit of their goals.

Someone who never gives up. Pushing yourself further than your limit. Someone who keeps pushing that wall back further and further. That is a beast.

LO: *What is your favorite book?*

SS: *Rich Dad Poor Dad,* by Robert Kiyosaki and Sharon Lechter. It's a fantastic book; I would recommend it to anyone.

LO: *What is your favorite exercise if you had twenty to thirty minutes and no weights?*

SS: Sprints if you have the space to run and burpees to tuck jumps. You have to go as hard as you possibly can in the time you have—that is the key.

LO: *What are you competing in now?*

SS: I have the second largest competition in Florida called the Crush Games. Then I have the largest competition in Florida called Wodapalooza. That will be in Bayfront Park with over fifteen hundred athletes representing thirty counties. It is an amazing competition. You can follow that on Twitter #WZAMiami.

LO: *When you hit a wall and want to quit a race, how do* *you overcome that feeling when you think you cannot go on anymore?*

SS: I speak to myself. I literally coach myself the same way I coach my students. Giving up is not an option. I need to replace any negative thoughts that sneak in with encouraging thoughts. "You can do this; you got this." Keep telling yourself this over and over again. Every time you conquer something, whether it is a big competition or a hard workout, you get stronger mentally. It then becomes who you are.

LO: *Do you drink alcohol?*

SS: I didn't drink for four years, but I'll have a drink socially every now and then. I will have a beer at one of the microbreweries that have been popping up. But all in all, I am not much of a drinker. I like to have fun, but I don't need to drink to have fun.

LO: *What is a piece of advice for someone who is stuck?*

SS: You can't hide from your fears or negative thoughts. You will need to tackle them. Deal with them. Take care of yourself. For me, it's getting into the gym first, then with a clear mind I can deal with my problems. Tackle any and all issues that come your way. Don't run from them—run toward them.

LO: *Where do you see yourself in the future?*

SS: I have such a passion for what I do, and I am lucky because I love helping people and pushing people to be their best. I will always be in the fitness business. I do see my boyfriend and me owning our own facility based on our workouts, shared visions, and philosophy of being beasts.

Don't judge a book by its cover. This five-foot firecracker—sorry, I mean M-80—will beat 99.9 percent of all men and women in any Spartan race on the planet. This #littlebeast is a monster when it comes to fitness. I want her on my team when the whistle blows in the game of life. Her focus, energy, and "no excuses" attitude are what it takes to be a beast. She brings out the beast in everyone who is lucky enough to know her.

PART TWO

ENTERING BEAST MODE

CHAPTER 4

SOCIAL INTELLIGENCE

"The highest wisdom is kindness."

PROVERB

Nothing in life happens without good social skills. You can call it selling, social intelligence, or the gift of gab, but when deals happen, promotions are awarded, and negotiations end favorably, it's due to good interpersonal skills. Harness the skills you already possess, and then study people as if it were a science to further improve upon them. Sales sometimes gets a bad rap, but everyone—regardless of profession—is a salesman at heart. You are selling yourself, the CEO of your own life. Those who succeed in our complex and often complicated world communicate well.

The golden rule of social intelligence is the ability to see the situation from the other person's perspective. If you can develop the skill of detaching yourself from the situation you're in and viewing it from the client's, the friend's, or the family member's perspective, you'll get to the heart of what he or she needs and be able to go from there. By gaining that insight, you will be able to solve problems and diffuse many arguments before they start. Detaching yourself will save you from wasting energy.

There are certain qualities you want to look for when surrounding yourself with the right people. I like people who see things for what they are with no smoke and mirrors; they tell it how it is, and they speak from their gut. You've got to be able to sense the difference between somebody who's fake and somebody who's real. The better you get at reading people, the better your defense mechanism becomes in avoiding toxic individuals.

I've never met a funny person who I didn't like. People who make you laugh are good to be around because laughing releases serotonin in your brain, and you want to be around people who make you feel good.

Avoid negative people at all costs. Negativity is contagious and disastrous. Negative people will kill your drive and veer you off track. It only takes one negative person to drag you or even your whole team down. His or her venom will hit you as if a cobra struck you, and that negativity will spread like cancer. Once you identify the seed of negativity in a team, the only way to protect the team from being infected is to cut that cancer-like negativity out.

As a manager early on in my career, I confronted a young advisor who brought negativity into the office, which began to infect all those around him. I watched as morale dropped and performance suffered. I gave him a chance to explain why I should keep him and asked him to write me a detailed letter explaining how he would change his attitude. He submitted the letter, explaining that he understood the problem and that he would fix it—but he didn't. Not too long after that, I let him go. Once he was removed and the negativity with him, things within the team returned back to normal. You have to have a zero tolerance policy for negativity, both in your personal life and business life.

EMULATE THE SUCCESSFUL

The flip side of the negativity coin is positive people in the form of quality mentors. It's important for you to find mentors. When I graduated college and first started out in the real world in 1997, I didn't have anyone to look up to or anyone whom I aspired to be like. Once I entered the financial world, I was suddenly surrounded by type A, hard-driving individuals I wanted to emulate. I knew if I worked hard and was given the guidance and the tools necessary, I could do anything. I could become the person I wanted to be because I had the right people to look up to and follow along a similar path.

People from all different fields and areas of expertise will come in and out of your life—teachers, rabbis, priests, entrepreneurs, coaches, lawyers—and each one of these encounters is an opportunity to learn. Depending on your values, your goals, and the vision for your life, you may need several mentors—the best of whom will form your personal board of directors. If businesses and nonprofits have a board of directors to move their respective mission and vision statements forward, so should we as humans. You are the CEO of your life, and you'll need a board of directors. Whether you want to tell these people that they have a special role in your life or not is entirely up to you, but they will give you knowledge and guidance in all aspects of life. Some will guide you spiritually, some through business affairs, and others through family life and relationships. You want to surround yourself with people who are going to lift you up and make you a better person. Sometimes tough love is necessary, so don't misconstrue that for negativity. There is a fine line between someone who is negative and someone who is being tough on you because you need it. "Better an honest slap than a false kiss."

“

I DESTROY MY ENEMIES WHEN I MAKE THEM MY FRIENDS.

”

ABRAHAM LINCOLN

In today's world, some of my greatest mentors are people I've never met. I've read their books, listened to their podcasts, watched their YouTube videos, or hit them up on Twitter. With the Internet, everything is at our fingertips. Want an answer to a question? Google it. Want access to the biggest beasts in your line of work? Search for them on YouTube. There's no excuse for not finding the right mentors. Use them not only for guidance but also for inspiration. Find your favorite author, and listen to his audiobooks. Browse Twitter, Snapchat, and Instagram stories, and follow billionaires or regular guys and girls sharing their tricks of the trade. I watch people such as Mark Cuban, 50 Cent, and Tai Lopez who have built businesses mentoring people on social media. I even follow young entrepreneurs such as fourteen-year-old Caleb Maddix, who randomly inspired me with his father on Periscope at 5:30 in the morning while I was walking my dog recently. There is so much out there right now, with more social platforms emerging every day. Whether you build a business off these platforms or just use them to connect, there is value out there. I can't begin to tell you the web of knowledge I've gained through the Internet over just the last six months that has dramatically altered my life for the better.

Your mentors should be a part of your daily life. In ancient times, the wealthiest would seek out and pay for philosophers such as Plato and Socrates—the brightest and most brilliant people of their era—to coach them on life. Today, that gift is given to you for free. Search for these modern-day philosophers; they are more than happy to share their knowledge with you. Take what you learn, and apply it immediately to your business and your life.

Whole communities and networks are being created online as we speak. The friendships and relationships you can develop through these networks create boundless business opportunities. I've developed deep and personal relationships with several mentors I found online and rekindled some old relationships, too. Because of Facebook, for example, a pledge brother who I knew in college twenty-two years ago was in Miami recently, and we spent a night together at a mixed martial arts cage-fighting event. It started out as a friendly union, but through conversations and catching up, he turned into a client. It's not the first time the power of social media reconnected me with an old friend or acquaintance and a business partnership was formed.

People who are ultrawealthy, ultrasuccessful, and ultrapowerful are usually more than happy to share their experiences and knowledge because it's fulfilling for them. Whether they write books, take time to be interviewed, or post various thoughts through their social media platforms, successful people like to share their knowledge. Plus—if you're lucky—they may make an investment in you or your idea. Don't be scared to ask someone in a powerful position how he or she got there. I like to say, "Drive to the hoop"—meaning, "Make your move."

After nearly twenty years in the financial world dealing with every personality type across the spectrum—from young, start-up entrepreneurs, to first-time millionaires, to billionaires and successful people in every profession—I've discovered that there really isn't a big difference among them. They're all human, they all bleed red, and their brains function in the same way as yours and mine. What did they do differently, then? They were the first ones in the office in the morning, they were the last ones to leave at night, and they ran that extra mile instead of quitting. They took extreme risks and didn't shy away from fear or uncertainty. By choosing to take on the hardest tasks—the ones no one else wanted to take on—and through discipline and hard work, they put themselves in a position to create their own luck.

You want to emulate the most successful people in your business and do what they did. What I like to do first is find books on them. If they offer a coaching program, jump at it and spend the money: it's a good investment. I cannot for the life of me understand how people can blow a few hundred dollars on dinner or drinks with friends but won't spend fifteen dollars on a book that can change their lives—or better yet, find the time to listen to a free podcast that will help them grow as people or in their businesses. Find a seminar or conference where the brightest and most successful people in your line of work will be, and spend that three hundred dollars to get there. Take notes, and soak it all up. This isn't an exercise to get down on yourself, either. At every level of any business, there is someone who is doing it better, and that should motivate you to take the extra steps to see how you can get there, too. And even if you only reach halfway, you'd still be better than where you started.

The end goal is to stick with people who are moving forward and avoid those who are dragging you down. Program yourself to be attracted toward finding people who can help you, and vice versa—people who make you laugh, and those you can make laugh; people you can trust, and those who trust you.

People exude a certain type of energy. When you meet someone, you should be able to decipher his or her character early on. There have been studies on this. You can feel and sense positive and negative energy because it radiates. When I worked at WorldCom helping people switch their phones lines and installing Internet access, I set up an appointment with a prospect at her company called Greens

Today. She was a struggling entrepreneur clawing her way to make just enough to survive and keep the doors open, yet her energy was unbelievably positive. The force of the energy I felt that day was something I never experienced before, and it made me want to find out more. She worked as a nutritionist, her business focused on healthy eating, and she was a student of Kabbalah. I became friends with her and even went to a couple Kabbalah classes. She gave me a book called *The Power of Kabbalah,* which I read pretty quickly and found to be uplifting and inspiring—sort of like Tony Robbins with a little spirituality sprinkled in. There was so much negativity in my life at the time that it was a real breath of fresh air, a gift out of nowhere. Your energy has a massive influence over the people around you in both a positive and negative way, so choose to be a person of light. ABP—meaning "always be positive"—was a unwritten rule of conduct around my office; there was just no time in the day for negativity. Do things that give you energy; don't do things that sap it.

The antithesis of the go-getter, a person who wants to strive for greatness and keep moving ahead, is the person who says, "You can't do that." While interning in college for a search engine company, before Google, I was told by one of the founders of the company (a fraternity brother and entrepreneur @luxurybarber), while riding down the elevator, "Life is like a bucket of crabs. As you are crawling out of that bucket, other crabs are trying to drag you back in." There will be times when even your closest friends seethe with jealousy as you start to do well, and they will drag you back into the "bucket." Don't let them. Don't feel guilty or bad. Keep moving forward and upward. You're getting out of the bucket, and they aren't. Do not take it personally, either. My own mother, who I can say loves me more than anyone in the world, would often tell me to get a regular job like everyone else and climb the corporate ladder. That was not who I was or wanted to be, so I refused to listen to her. Because I grew up with men in my life who were entrepreneurs and salesmen, it was in my DNA to carve my own path. It wasn't easy, and to this day it remains a daily battle to find the work/life balance of providing for my family and also being a present father and good husband.

Learn to identify people who may not have your best interest at heart, and don't let them stop you. Once you can identify these types, you can avoid their arrows and their crab claws trying to hold you down. When you find your own path and plug into what makes you tick, you'll become a spark of energy to other people, and they'll start noticing and being attracted to you.

When I began in finance, there were kids starting out in this field from every single walk of life: rich, middle class, and poor. Some were from Harvard and Princeton, some from broken homes, and some straight off the boat from Russia and Eastern Europe, but everyone started at the exact same point. The beauty of capitalism is none of those backgrounds mattered. It didn't matter if you had an accent; it didn't matter if you had a degree from an Ivy League school; it didn't matter if you came from an affluent home or a poor one. What differentiated those who succeeded with those who didn't was their ability to work hard and persevere. With my head down and my nose to the ground, the owners of my firm took notice of my "no excuses" type of work ethic and positive energy, and I was promoted to managing director in no time.

With my new title, I immediately headed to Barnes & Noble and purchased *One Minute Manager* by Kenneth Blanchard—which is still one of my all-time favorite books. Sharpening my leadership skills from then on became a lifelong passion. Leadership to me is defined as action. Leaders create their own space; they take charge of the meeting. No one is going to anoint you king; you must take leadership. The entrepreneur is the ultimate lone wolf. You must take it upon yourself to be all things. You must find the solution. To succeed you must become the smartest, the most humble, and the most resilient. You must never waiver. You must be willing to do all that it takes, whenever needed, without self-pity or complaining. You must face the odds and know that you will beat them. There is no plan B. Master leadership skills, and business will follow.

SOCIAL PRACTICES

Regardless of whether you're extroverted or introverted, bold or shy, talkative or quiet, there are various ways to practice your social skills. The first is simply to get out there. Get off your couch, even if you don't want to, and seek people out. Nobody will give you business or hire you if you're not engaging. This life is a contact sport. The more contacts you make, the better off you'll be. People are not going to knock on your door if they don't know what you do, so you need to get out and create relationships. I can't stand networking, but I love building relationships. This doesn't happen overnight, either. It takes time, diligence, persistence, and consistency.

Go to conferences and meet like-minded people as often as you can. It's essential to have an action plan when attending social functions for business. What's the goal? Is it to garner new clients? To listen to a mentor speak? Who do you want to meet? Are you going for deal making? Are you doing a reconnaissance mission where you're going to gather information to help you make decisions in your business? Or are you going just for fun to take a personal day and learn? Even if you're going to have fun, be cognizant that you're always building your brand. You want to do a little homework on any event you plan on attending to make sure your goals will be reached. When I go to a specific conference for financial advisors or traders, I research and find out who will be there. Doing so helps me find my purpose in attending. Do I identify with any of these people? To whom do I need to make an effort to find and introduce myself? With whom can I build a relationship?

Once you've put in the time to attend functions, expos, and conferences, people will start talking about you and seeking you out. Maybe they need your skills, advice, or expertise. Find things that pique your interest, and invest the time and money—the payback will be worth it.

When I moved to Florida, I started playing tennis, and it became a passion; I loved it with all my heart and soul. At first, none of the better players in the club (I like to call them tennis snobs) wanted to play with me since I wasn't on their level. I invested in some lessons, and within one year, I made the 4.5 team with the best players—who became my good friends—and competed in high-level competitions. My passion and love for tennis over the past ten years created not just friendships but also lifelong clients. When you have passions and other people share those passions, they're more likely to do business with you because like attracts like—beasts attract beasts. On that same note, my best friend when I was growing up is now the right-hand man to a major trucking company. He landed a job because he was the owner's doubles partner in a men's tennis league. I won't be surprised if one day he owns the company. Don't discount the networking that can be done within the things you enjoy.

Another social skill is to track your image. The way you dress, the way you look, and the way you carry yourself is the first thing others notice, and they will judge and evaluate you. Even if you're not making a lot of money, save up and purchase a nice suit, a nice tie, and a nice pair of shoes. They don't have to be expensive, but be sure to keep them clean, pressed, and polished. People shouldn't "judge a book by its cover," but they do—that's just the reality. In my line of work—just like in many other professional fields—whether you like it or not, people are going to be attracted to you if you smell and you look like you're successful. Do not underestimate the power of dressing the part, because it makes good impressions, and when you're meeting people who can potentially contribute to achieving your goals, impressions are important.

I'll let you in on a little secret, regardless of whether you're a beginner or seasoned professional: Dress, speak, and act not for who you are but who you want to be. Regardless of what it is, "act as if." Act *as if* you are already successful. Being successful starts in your mind. Act *as if* you are the best in your line of work. When you exude confidence, people are more receptive to you and what you have to offer. If you're a general contractor pulling up in a Ford F-150 wearing a hardhat, jeans, and a T-shirt, that is your role, so play it well and do so with confidence. I want my painter to be in overalls with paint stains, arriving on time, and parking his van in the driveway. I want my lawyer looking sharp as a sword with notebook in hand. You get the point. Whatever you do, put on that uniform and come to win. I am not that good at golf, but when I golf, I look like I am the best golfer on the course (and I therefore play better).

Your image extends to social media avenues, too. The photos and status updates you post, the pages you like, and how you engage with others are all available for the public (i.e., potential clients) to see and judge you. Be cognizant of your online persona; it's just as important as your physical one.

Once you're an active participant in your community (business or otherwise), you'll undoubtedly establish new contacts, make a few new friends, and create new relationships. Once you have grown your circle of influence, you can start organizing events and converting these relationships into clients or mentors. If they're looking for business, they'll refer business to you because they like you, trust you, and feel comfortable with you.

In addition to any face-to-face and in-person events, another simple way of putting yourself out there is to engage with others on social media. Start with simply wishing a happy birthday on Facebook or congratulating someone on an achievement via LinkedIn. Through these simple acts, you maintain contact with people who might be of value to you down the line. Expanding your reach on social media will create the greatest payback for the least amount of effort. Even if you're currently employed or aren't looking for prospects, take the small amount of time it takes to stay engaged with the people in your social networks—you never know what opportunities may arise. I've had a great return in garnering clients and expanding my professional network by doing these simple things. I love reaching out and asking questions on Twitter. It feels good to wish a buddy whom you haven't seen in twenty-five years a happy birthday. It feels good to congratulate an old colleague on a new job promotion on LinkedIn. Don't discount how a simple gesture has the potential to change your life forever.

The last tip on perfecting the art of social intelligence is a nonverbal tip from Mother Nature: God gave us two ears and one mouth so as to speak rarely and listen often. The best in business are those who shut up and listen. While it sounds relatively easy, it's not. Given the chance, most people talk endlessly about themselves. As a good listener, let them. I challenge you to listen more and speak less with each person in your life—family members, strangers, clients, and so on. People who are good listeners and show interest in others are the ones who leave the best impressions.

As an entrepreneur, it's imperative to gather as much information as you can—this could be about the business itself, those in it, competitors, and so on. Practice asking open-ended questions and then listening; it's a fantastic technique to get to know the needs and desires of your clients. If you're genuinely interested and engaged, they will open up and give you amazing amounts of information. You can learn a lot about a person in a matter of a few questions. Open-ended questions can lead to an amazing array of information—perhaps the potential sale of a house, the need for a mortgage, or a CD rolling due. Any and all information gained through the use of proper questions will give you the ability to strike while the iron is hot and potentially land some business. The possibilities are endless, and you wouldn't know unless you took the time to invest in some social intelligence gathering.

There is, however, a fine line between the art of conversation and being annoying. No one wants to feel as if she is being interrogated. Your number-one currency is how you make someone else feel. If that person feels comfortable around you, he will open up. If not, you will need to earn his trust.

As a financial advisor, my business is evolving and constantly changing. It's not just about giving financial advice anymore; it's about having a deep relationship with my clients. All of them can call me with anything regarding their lives or livelihood twenty-four hours a day, seven days a week, 365 days a year—and I make sure they understand that. Knowing as much as I can about my clients is vital to the advice I give. I made a big change in how I conducted business in 2001 after the markets crashed; I vowed never to become a commissioned broker again. For me, that was the turning point. I was charging commission to buy and sell—at that time, this was the norm, like a real-estate broker charging a commission to buy and sell—but I changed my business model and I became a fee-based financial advisor where I sat on the same side of the table with my clients and became their partner. It is very important, in dealing with people and in relationships, that there is transparency and trust. In life, the goal should always be to find a win-win solution for all parties. My job is to detach myself and put myself in my client's shoes and ask, "Would I want to be hearing that advice?"

If the answer to that question is yes, then I'm on the right track.

INTERVIEW WITH JOCKO WILLINK

While writing this book, I listened to a Tim Ferris podcast and a Joe Rogan podcast in which each interviewed Jocko Willink. Do yourself a favor and Google Jocko Willink, and get ready to be blown away. Jocko coauthored a book with Leif Babin called *Extreme Ownership: How U.S. Navy SEALs Lead and Win.* Jocko and Leif served together in SEAL Task Unit Bruiser, the most highly decorated special operations unit from the war in Iraq. Their efforts contributed to the historic triumph for US forces in Ramadi. Jocko spent twenty years in the US Navy SEAL Teams, starting as an enlisted SEAL and rising through the ranks to become a SEAL officer. During his career, Jocko was awarded the Silver Star, the Bronze Star, and numerous other personal and unit awards. In 2010, Jocko retired from the navy and launched Echelon Front where he teaches the leadership principles he learned on the battlefield to help others lead and win.

Jocko is the definition of a beast. Soon after the Tim Ferris interview, he launched his own podcast, which quickly became my favorite. If you're like me and like war stories combined with leadership advice, life advice, and a bit of jiu-jitsu sprinkled in, then download Jocko's podcast.

Our friendship started on Twitter, where he is active answering people's questions. I recently returned from the first ever #Muster001, a one-of-a-kind conference geared toward leaders who want to dominate their battlefield. Jocko and Leif dove deep into the concepts of #ExtremeOwnership and how to build, train, and lead high-performance, winning teams. I spent two days in San Diego, waking up at 4:45 a.m. to revile with a few hundred hard-core troopers. Jocko was gracious enough to take time out and do an interview me. Like everything he does in his life, he gets straight to the point. Jocko is one of the most down-to-earth, nicest guys I've ever met. With that said, I would not want to piss him off. You can follow him @jockowillink on Twitter, Instagram, and Facebook.

LO: *If you were told to grab one book only for a long trip, what book would you choose?*

JW: *About Face: The Odyssey of an American Warrior* by Colonel David H. Hackworth.

LO: *How many hours of sleep do you get a night? What advice do you have for someone who did not get a good night's sleep and can't focus or make good decisions because he or she feels so tired?*

JW: I sleep around five and a half hours a night. Feeling tired? Do some burpees, or at least some push-ups.

LO: *What is the most important character trait you look for in a person?*

JW: Humility.

LO: *Can you define what a beast means to you?*

JW: A beast is someone, bordering on something, that can't be stopped.

LO: *Are you born a beast, or can you learn how to become one?*

JW: Some people are born beasts. Some people become beasts.

LO: *If you can give one piece of advice to a young man or woman who felt down, stuck, or depressed, what would you tell him or her to do?*

JW: Get undepressed. Own your life. Own your future. Do what must be done. GET AFTER IT.

I have a deep respect and appreciation for Navy SEALs, Army Rangers, Air Force, Marines—anyone who has served or is currently serving to protect civilians in this great country. Although we will face a variety of battles in our personal lives, most of us will never see an actual battlefield where we lay our life on the line. This next chapter is dedicated to the real warriors who voluntarily enlist in the military to protect and serve our country. To the men and women of the armed services who risk their lives to defend our freedom, thank you!

CHAPTER 5

THE WARRIOR MIND-SET

"We have before us an ordeal of the most grievous kind. We have before us many, many long months of struggle and of suffering. You ask, what is our policy? I can say: It is to wage war, by sea, land and air, with all our might and with all the strength that God can give us; to wage war against a monstrous tyranny, never surpassed in the dark, lamentable catalogue of human crime. That is our policy. You ask, what is our aim? I can answer in one word: It is victory, victory at all costs, victory in spite of all terror, victory, however long and hard the road may be; for without victory, there is no survival."

WINSTON CHURCHILL

Of all the tools you have at your disposal, the mind is the most important. The warrior mind-set is my favorite way to have the mind of a beast. Some have a natural ability to think strategically, while others have to learn how. Many beasts throughout history have lived life with the mind-set of a strategic warrior.

DEVELOPING THE WARRIOR MIND-SET

As a kid, like all the other boys in my neighborhood, I loved to play war. Whether it was laser tag, paintball, or war video games, I was always drawn to games with a warlike aspect. Chess, football, poker, hockey, soccer, and even the card game "War" were among my favorites. Why? Because they are all simulated versions of war where strategy and tactics determine the winner and the loser.

There are many books that deal with war and the warrior mentality. My favorite books are *33 Strategies of War* by Robert Greene, *Art of War* by Sun Tzu, and *The Book of Five Rings* by Miyamoto Musashi (the greatest swordsman in Japan). These books lay out the many strategies of war—timeless relics of information that can be applied in any boardroom, business transaction, or decision.

Warriors completely commit themselves—their minds, bodies, and souls—to their vision and mission in life. In order to do that, however, a warrior must make daily sacrifices. These sacrifices include developing a set of attitudes that reign above all others. Everything a warrior does will revolve around these principles. It is called the warpath.

Regardless of what you do for a living—whether you're a doctor, lawyer, or financial advisor—acquire the best tools and technology you can afford. Build your war chest with what's needed to win. If you need to take out a loan, do so if the return on investment is worth it. Cash reserves will be important for setbacks and delays. In the war room, you will need all the ammunition necessary to win your battles. Computers, smartphones, software, laptops, gifts, thank-you notes, briefings, and compliance rules are all examples. Do not cheap out on the necessities that will help you grow. If your competitors have it, you better have a damn good reason why you don't. Make sure your environment is conducive to working at a peak state. The one thing that can't be bought is your passion and skill set that you bring to the table.

Having a warrior mind-set means having a positive focus about your mission and demonstrating the appropriate behavior to back it up. I often look back and think about what it must have been like for my grandfather who, as an eight-year-old boy, along with his ten-year-old brother, fled Russia on a boat to come to this country. I wonder what it must have been like for a family rounded up in

Nazi-controlled Europe, or fleeing famine in Ireland, or escaping fascism in Italy. People throughout history and today live with insurmountable conflict and stress. Many of these individuals survived by having a warrior mind-set, focusing on survival.

What about all the immigrants who came through Ellis Island and landed in America with nothing? Most of the people who built America were immediately forced into a warrior mind-set because it meant their survival and often that of their families. Take the Israelis, for example, who rebuilt their country out of the ashes of the Holocaust. I gain strength from those who overcame hardship despite the odds against them. I try to put myself in their shoes, at ground zero, and think about how they persevered.

Reading or watching stories of the men and women who fought and continue to fight to keep us safe from dictators and terrorists inspires me. Read their stories for inspiration.

Find a person (or group of people) you can relate with who succeeded against all odds, and read about it. It is a powerful practice. You can build whatever you want with the right mind-set.

Most humans have a warrior mentality—or are at least

capable of developing one—because it comes from our basic instincts of survival. We obviously don't have the same threats as our Paleolithic brothers and sisters, but we can—and should—tap into our survivor consciousness to help guide us through life's curveballs.

Unfortunately, college doesn't teach us much about making it in the "real world"—what I call survivor consciousness. I don't think the majority of kids are prepared for the real world after graduating college. Most of us struggled in the first year or two (sometimes longer) with this new, unknown world. Survivor consciousness is basically what happens at "death ground," defined as a place when your back is against the wall, the water is behind you, the enemy is coming to attack, and you have to fight like hell to survive. In my opinion, there should be a mandated class for every college kid called Death Ground 101.

If you don't do anything to develop it, your survivor mentality will surface at some point in your life. I was lucky; it happened to me early when I was twenty-two years old. For some, it happens at age forty when they get fired from their job and have a family to support. For others, it's going to happen even later. Survivor consciousness will surface when you enter a state of mind where you are broken financially, spiritually, and intellectually—you can't think straight, nothing is going right, and things are falling apart around you. This is when your survivor instinct kicks in, and it's time to dig yourself out.

The key in the face of adversity is to remain calm. Defeat is a learning experience. Once you've successfully dug yourself out, a warrior is born and that survivor consciousness doesn't leave you. This mind-set is especially beneficial if you're an entrepreneur. For a salesman who is 100 percent in charge of his own paycheck, survivor consciousness is a constant state of mind.

When you're operating your own business, unexpected things happen, and things change quickly. Your mind-set will help you adapt quickly to the changes and help you continue onward. This brings me back to the lone-wolf economy and taking charge of your own destiny. You have to commit, trust your own gut, and take responsibility for the decisions you've made. You are the general in your own war. The best generals in the world lead from the front. Study people like Napoleon Bonaparte, probably the greatest general of all time. He was a soldier's soldier. Leaders are people who take risks and are boldly on the frontlines. *Fortune favors the bold.* Being bold is projecting confidence—both in yourself and in your work. People respect those who make a stand because a lot of people are guided by fear. They're scared to ask questions, to make decisions, or to stand up for what they believe in. Your

“

A VIOLENT MIND WIELDS A CARELESS SWORD.

”

MIYAMOTO MUSASHI

decisions may not always be right, but as long as you're making decisions based on intelligence and your experience, and with good intentions, people respect that, and success will follow suit. The more you practice being bold, the more it will become second nature.

Once you're engaged with your work, think of yourself as a sniper—stay focused, in the zone, and avoid pointless distractions. This is not a time for personal phone calls. Respect those focused individuals, and do not rob them of their precious time—you are stealing money out of their pockets. Do not take personally their reaction to you, either; learn from their example. They're whom you want to emulate. There will be plenty of time to shoot the shit, have a cocktail, and share some laughs later.

Develop a strategy to deal with distractions and anyone trying to take you out of your zone. When you watch professional athletes, Olympians, and elite performers compete, it's as if they're the only ones in the universe. When the whistle blows, there could be 50,000 fans in the stadium cheering and screaming, and they won't hear a thing because their warrior mind-set is solely focused on the task before them.

Thinking like a warrior does not mean constantly asserting dominance or looking for fights. Quite the contrary—you're looking to inspire, guide, and be a good role model, especially if you're working on a team. I believe in leading from the front. It's how I always operated and managed: not so much through words but through deeds. People respect and listen to those who either are doing it or have done it. I want to be led by someone who has been to war, smelled the smoke, and fought on the frontlines, not by someone who has only read a book about war. If I am taking advice from someone about business, I want to know that they, too, have been there, done that. Everyone has an opinion, but those who lead by example are the most admired. I would never ask someone to do something that I haven't already done or was not willing to do myself.

The warrior mind-set is very serious, especially in regard to making decisions about business and money. Starting and running a business is risky, and with risk come consequences—severe ones if you're not clearheaded during your daily battles. A brain surgeon doing his best to save a cancer patient has more in common with a marine on the frontlines than you can imagine. What is the common thread? The warrior mind-set. In both cases, one wrong move can lead to death.

A lot of warrior strategies overlap with social intelligence, which we discussed in the last chapter. In business and in life, you have to weave through the maze of people and keep a keen eye on what their motivations might be. Whether they want to take your hard work and try to profit from it or whether they are sincere in their word, you will encounter all sorts of human interactions; so be levelheaded, and don't take things personally. Be confident in yourself, and don't let your ego get in the way of your mission.

You need to know which traits to look for in other people and use them to identify who are friends and who are foes. It is a very slippery road to navigate through, whether you are an entrepreneur or you are working for someone else. You need to survey those around you and understand their needs, motivations, and desires. When you're in business, you're dealing with clients, partners, and employees—all of whom have their own lives with their own objectives. Dealing with each should not be difficult as long as you follow some simple steps.

STAY ABOVE THE COMPETITION

Whether you're a financial advisor, a lawyer, a realtor, a doctor, a dentist, an accountant, or anything else, it's your duty to separate yourself from your competition and get your story out; no one will do it for you. You are the captain of your own ship.

General George S. Patton and General Erwin Rommel were two tacticians who fought against each other during some of the most crucial battles during World War II. When later asked how they prepared for battle, they both responded: "I read whatever I could get my hands on to get into the mind of my opponent." They both wanted to understand the mind of the enemy, to figure out how the other thinks in order to gain some sort of strategic edge for the battle. That could be applied to business as well. When dealing with other people, try to see what they see. Once you're able to do that, you can avoid some pitfalls or fights, and you'll know when to retreat and when to engage. Try and figure out what makes a person tick. All businesses deal with clients, so understanding who your client is will be essential for your success. You also have to know your competition and be likeable so as to attract clients to you and away from your competition.

There are thousands of other financial advisors out there. It is my job to get inside the investor's mind psychologically and financially to understand exactly what this individual expects and wants out of the relationship. It is my job to devise the game plan so that my clients can reach their goals. People often do business with those they like, whether hiring a real-estate broker or lawyer or finding a doctor or dentist. Businesses grow primarily according to the likability of the proprietor. People become return customers because of the way the business and its associates made them feel. In my business, as someone who is privy to and in charge of a person's financial secrets, I need to develop skills that make my clients feel comfortable, safe, and confident with me.

As a lone wolf in the world we live in today, you must become an expert in the battlefield you operate in. You are the Navy SEAL commando operating for the commander in chief, your client. You must separate yourself from your competition with something unique. Think about who needs your skills, and approach them. My strategic advantage is the relationships I have cultivated with my clients and made a priority.

FORM STRATEGIC RELATIONSHIPS

As you operate on your own battlefield, be sure to constantly meet people, build your team, and seek individuals who have a good heart, have good intentions, and have a positive influence on you. These are your allies. At the end of the day, we are all searching for people we want on our team. The people you keep in your life are part of your team, your army, and your intelligence agency. Build your army for life's battles. You never know when you may need to call on one of them for a job, some motivation, or a major project that needs to be completed. My code in life is simple. Help a friend, be a friend, use your brain, and don't let fear win. Do the best you can do at the task you are given, keep moving, and help people. It's that simple. You will grow your network, build your allies, and live a good life.

“

WITH SELF-DISCIPLINE MOST ANYTHING IS POSSIBLE.

”

THEODORE ROOSEVELT

DEAL CAREFULLY WITH ENEMIES

Having an enemy in your line of work or business is a good thing. We should never create enemies on purpose or actively seek them out, but when they come—and believe me, they will come—be ready to confront those situations and deal with them head-on. Without getting angry and losing your temper, you should strategically outmaneuver this individual or group of individuals.

When I started in finance, my fraternity brother from college who helped me get into finance turned on me. We had always had a good relationship, but we were also two competitive, type A personalities. As the growth in my business started to accelerate, I sensed a bit of animosity. For whatever reason, darts were thrown, arrows were slung, and one day he came at me like a lion. I was uncertain as to why, but at that point, I didn't care. I drew the line and declared war in my mind. I certainly wasn't going to take any shit from him. In the world of business, we don't fight with fists or guns; we fight with strategy. Our friendship ended, and we stopped speaking to one another for years. He drove my level of success and motivated me like nothing else could. It was one of the greatest things that happened to me because it lit a fire in my belly that may not have been there otherwise.

If you look at businesses around the country, there are

several competing companies: Starbucks versus Dunkin' Doughnuts, Coke versus Pepsi, IBM versus Microsoft, Facebook versus Twitter, and so on. Sports would be boring if it wasn't for competition between athletes or sports teams: Ali versus Frasier, Larry Bird versus Magic Johnson, New York Yankees versus New York Mets, Conor McGregor versus Nate Diaz—the list goes on and on. Whenever you have two competing forces, they will always make one another better. As for the little rivalry with my fraternity brother, I'm happy to have him back as an ally and close friend.

At the end of Steve Jobs's life, Bill Gates stopped by his house, and they spoke about many things, patching up old wounds. The rivalry bordering on absolute hatred between Steve Jobs and Bill Gates drove each of them to want to win. Later they both understood that it was not really a personal feud, but the fuel to keep the fires lit within each company. Competition is a good thing; it elevates the desire to succeed. Competition among companies keeps them engaged, always striving to improve and be better. Consumers get higher-end products because companies are competing for their spending dollars. In the end, everyone wins.

You'll have many encounters that may cause friction. Some of those people might be your best friends, offering friendly criticism to help you improve; and others are just out to hurt you and want you to fail. Enemies can come in different forms. Some come head-on, like my fraternity brother, but the more dangerous ones operate covertly behind the scenes to take you down. Keep your eyes and ears open for those you suspect to have ulterior motives, and steer clear of them.

Another motivating factor that helped me reach higher levels in my line of work was the desire to prove myself to those who doubted me. Success is the greatest revenge for those who might have abandoned you. A winner is a loser who got pissed off and worked to prove everyone wrong. Learn to love competition and embrace anyone who wants to challenge you. You will come out of it better, faster, and stronger.

INTERVIEW WITH DAVE DZIEKANSKI

Dave Dziekanski is a New York City native, born and bred in the heart of Manhattan. Dave and I worked together not too long ago, and he is one of the nicest human beings I've ever met. When I needed a solution for clients who wanted to have a more tactical approach to investing, Dave was the guy I talked to. Dave is a numbers guy and a math whiz armed with a degree in applied mathematics and a master's of science in finance, and he agreed with me about the need for some quant-based solutions for clients investing in a computerized world.

The Dave I once knew was a big, 290-pound guy. Dave today is a 180-pound Spartan racer who tears up the New York City gym circuit while angel investing and managing portfolios. I wanted to know how he made the change to become a beast, so I phoned up my business partner and friend to pick his brain.

LO: *Why did you get into fitness, and what caused the switch to shed 110 pounds?*

DD: I started feeling unhealthy and lethargic, but the key moment that sticks out in my mind was when I was on a ski trip with my friends and I just could not move the way I wanted to. The switch went off in my head; I needed to lose weight. I also went through a life transformation when my grandfather and my father passed away that same summer. My grandfather was a health nut who lived a long and healthy life; my dad, not so much. This was a spiritual awakening for me, so I had a decision to make. I was going to get myself in shape and be healthy.

LO: *What is one thing you are better at than anyone else?*

DD: I believe that would be my analytic skills—my ability to make connections other people may not be able to see. I am able to assess a situation and find the solution, whether that is in a social dynamic or a math problem.

LO: *How many hours of sleep do you need?*

DD: Seven.

LO: *Do you drink alcohol?*

DD: I'm a social drinker. Clear liquor or wine. Just a glass or two.

LO: *What is your favorite exercise?*

DD: The megaformer, which is a Pilates machine on steroids.

It will shred you up quickly with an amazing total-body workout. I also enjoy jump rope, row machine, swimming, yoga, and any interval training.

LO: *You physically transformed into a new person. What would you tell someone who was stuck in a place he or she was not happy in?*

DD: I believe when people see a big change or project, they become frozen with fear of failing, so they never start it. That is the major problem. Take that first step; whether you fail or not is irrelevant. What is important is the first step. Nothing is obtained inconsistently; you need to work for it every day. Look at the project as something that never ends, and enjoy it. The first step will be the hardest, but every day you don't take that step, you will fall deeper and deeper into your hole. Take one step each day, and slowly but surely you will get yourself into a new place, physically and mentally. Take the plunge.

LO: *You eat clean, but do you still have a burger once in a while? Cookies? Or popcorn?*

DD: Yeah, every once in a while. Everything in moderation.

LO: What is your favorite book?

DD: *Freakonomics* by Stephen Dubner and Steven Leavitt.

LO: *What races have you completed?*

DD: I've done a three-in-a-half-mile Spartan sprint race, a sixteen-mile Spartan race on a ski mountain with thirty-four obstacles (and finished top 20 percent), an eight-mile Spartan race, and a tough mudder.

LO: *I am looking to do my first Spartan race. Got any tips?*

DD: Write down the date, sign up for the race, and then you are committed. You have to sign up first—that is my tip.

Watching Dave transform himself from overweight to Spartan beast, competing in the hardest races in the country, is truly amazing. It goes to show that whatever you put your mind to, you can accomplish. Don't be scared to do it. Dave is an all-around example, and I look forward to hitting the gym with him and partnering with him in future businesses.

CHAPTER 6

SPIRITUALITY

"Excellence is the result of caring more than one may think is wise, risking more than what is considered safe, dreaming more than one may think is practical, expecting more than one may think is possible. Excellence is the seed of our breath."

UNKNOWN

I don't want to misconstrue this chapter as a religious chapter because spirituality can be many things. I consider myself spiritual, but in my own, personal way. There are many different rivers that lead to the same ocean, and how you get to that ocean is up to you—as long as the ocean leads to a place of good intentions. Recognize that the journey is the prize. The time-tested saying "Do unto others as you would want done to you" is the golden standard that we should each strive to live by, regardless of where you look for sage advice. To me, spirituality represents the subconscious mind—your inner self—and how it aligns with making good decisions and having a good heart. It's about finding a higher purpose than the materialistic self.

Spirituality will come into play when you encounter obstacles that look insurmountable or when life deals you its hardest trials and setbacks. You'll fall back on your spirituality when you don't know what to do, have no answers, and are searching for wisdom. For some, that might mean going to church or temple. To others, that might mean a walk in the woods or meditation. Whatever it is, having a connection will help you find the light during life's darkness.

I had a spiritual awakening after the market crash of 2000. This was a frightening time for me, and I needed to make some changes immediately. The absolute first thing I realized was the need to sit on the same side of the table with my clients, not across from them, and eliminate any conflicts of interest while representing them wholeheartedly. This decision also meant I would make less money, but that didn't matter, because my clients' interests took priority. Once you put the needs of your clients first, your business will grow exponentially. Don't worry about how you're going to get paid. Instead, worry about how you're going to take care of the person who trusts you.

You can also think of spirituality as a "searching mode" where you search for purpose and meaning. If you're experiencing something that's stressing you out, look at it as the universe's way of saying, "You are off track, and you need to change something."

Think of it as a flashlight shining light on an area you need to work on or correct. This should help you move in the direction toward achieving your goals that you outlined earlier in your vision. Stress is an indicator, a fire alarm in your subconscious signaling that something needs to be changed. Figure out what it is, and once you make a change, the pressure will disappear. Action alleviates anxiety. Don't be afraid of tension. Instead, tackle it and learn from it; when you do so, the outcome will be positive. It's through dark periods that we learn to appreciate the light and the beauty that life has to offer. Once we hit stress (or any challenging obstacle), we have two choices: to be reactive or to be proactive. A reactive response would be a defensive one full of excuses, avoidance, and finger-pointing—traits we despise in other people. Don't be that person. Own your mistakes; own your situations. A proactive response would be an offensive one where you attack the problem and deal with it step by step.

A beast is always driven.

If you're having trouble at work, be proactive. What can you do to improve the situation? Talk to your boss, ask questions, avoid negative employees, and so on. If you're having trouble with your marriage, be proactive and talk to your spouse. Go see a therapist together. Dedicate time to address the issue, create a plan, and then implement it. If your child is misbehaving at school or not doing well, don't raise your voice. Find a solution, and act on it. Reacting to it without a plan will only lead you to more problems.

You might be familiar with the saying "No pain, no gain." In the gym, it means to deal with the suffering and sweat today so you can see the payback and reward later. In business, the discomfort of long hours of hard work won't be seen until later. Sometimes you have to really go through some tough situations in order to achieve something that takes you to a higher level of consciousness and, ultimately, a better life. It's through these situations that we learn our greatest lessons.

From a spiritual standpoint, people tend to want to share and give back whenever they can to help others. You might not be financially able to help, but what you can always give is your time. You can give by being there for someone going through tough times, actively listening, or making

“

SILENCE IS A SOURCE OF GREAT STRENGTH.

”

LAO TZU

beneficial connections to help that person. At times, I think that's even better than giving financially, especially since the energy from beasts is infectious and contagious, and it'll spread to those you're trying to help.

Be wary of a person, however, who is experiencing constant problems or struggles and who expects your help or attention and then grows upset when you don't give it to him or her. Like anything in this world, you have only so many resources and so much time to give. Don't let someone drain you to the point where you can't give to yourself and your family. There's a fine line between being helpful and being an enabler to someone who just won't listen. Don't let someone suck your energy.

Time in our life is the only thing in the world you cannot get back, so be extremely sensitive to what you're doing with it. There's nothing wrong with being a little selfish. Don't feel bad when you can't give or share, because you only have so much energy and time in a day to do so. You might want to set aside a certain portion of your day for charity. Some people give 10 percent of their income, and that's great if you have the means to give. If you don't, give 10 percent of your time to causes you believe in. Give what you can without expecting to receive anything in return. Do it from your heart.

I use a metaphor when I think about the spiritual mentality of a beast, and I briefly mentioned it in the introduction of this book. We all have two beasts inside of us: a blue one and a red one. The blue one represents the good beast, the one who makes all the right decisions that lead to happiness. The blue beast wants to get out of bed early, is excited to tackle the day, and is looking for ways to be a force of good in the world. The red one represents the opposite. The red beast represents the nastiness inside of you and the lack of focus that takes you away from your goals. In business, the blue beast stands by clients and understands them as friends; the red one looks at them as transactions and tries to take advantage of them. In life, the blue beast is constantly going out of his comfort zone; the red one stays lethargic and lazy. You can call it whatever you want, but the red beast is your own enemy, your internal competitor, and your opponent. The red beast manifests in many ways: when stress takes over, when depression kicks in, when anger surfaces and you say the wrong things—words hurt like being cut with a knife. Understand that's when your red beast is having a field day. It's your responsibility to keep your red beast in check.

You can apply this metaphor to anything—take eating healthy, for example. The red beast wants the sugar in coffee, a six-pack of Dunkin' Donuts, and a shake for desert; the blue beast knows to resist. If your goal is to lose weight and eat healthy, that blue beast better be strong enough to win against the donut-craving red beast. If you're goal is to pay off debt, the red beast is going to want a shopping spree while the blue beast knows better. This battle between blue versus red is something we all internally struggle with daily. Entering beast mode is about winning those daily internal battles so you can go out and win the battles in life. The end result is living your life to its fullest potential and enjoying every aspect of your family, your friendships, your business, and yourself.

Everything we've talked about leading up to this chapter deals with feeding the blue beast and keeping that red beast at bay. You will inevitably lose some battles, so don't beat yourself up over it. Make sure your goals are realistic, and it'll be easier to contain that red beast.

That red beast is part of who you are. You don't want to kill the red beast; you just want to tame it like a wild horse—you want to control it.

A good friend who I played tennis with recently told me that he hasn't been playing because he was frustrated with his performance. I told him he's letting his red beast win. He was letting the little devil in his head stop him from playing the game he loves! I explained we all have this internal red beast inside of us who is our own worst enemy. That red beast is our true opponent whom we battle every day to avoid succumbing to defeat. In the game of life, you're playing against your opponent every day. You have to fight through your own internal struggles and not be so hard on yourself.

This enemy inside all of us will never go away. We are human, so we doubt ourselves, we question our ability, and we often settle. You beat it by following the strategies in this book, as well as those strategies that you'll gain from your own life experiences. Life will hit you hard; it's how you deal with it that separates the warriors from the worriers.

The red beast has to exist so the blue beast can grow stronger. That red beast is always just around the corner, looking to pick a fight. A beast is always at war with himself, but the more you practice taming your own internal opponent, the better you will get at it.

This sounds like a lot of work, and I'm not going to lie—it is. Being a beast isn't about floating around life with no direction or purpose. People who have real callings are able to commit—to the vision, to the goals, to battling the red beast—every day. Each of us has a calling; you just have to find it. I believe every person has a gift, and tapping into that talent is essential. You might even have multiple talents. If you do, you have the luxury of picking the one you like best. Or perhaps one talent is stronger than the others. My true strength is seeing things as they are and not what I wish them to be. I like to see things from all angles and convey that message clearly to clients and/or friends. That is my strength. I take the vision and let others do the executing. I tapped into my talents, and I'm using them in a positive, productive, and fulfilling manner.

Something strange happened to me when I was fifteen years old. For whatever reason, I was cold-called by a financial advisor who began to pitch me on a stock idea. I was completely intrigued by the experience. I asked the random caller if he liked what he did for a living, and he responded by telling me that it was challenging but that he did enjoy it. I eventually told him I was only fifteen years old with no money to invest, but that I appreciated the phone call; and we hung up. Looking back now, that very well could have been a sign from a higher power because eight years later, I became that guy.

If you have multiple talents, know that you can't do everything; it's difficult to wear multiple hats and expect to produce quality work.

Humans evolve, and things are constantly changing, so you must be able to change and evolve quickly, too. You can't be stagnant and remain the person you were a week

“

YOUR SPIRIT IS THE TRUE SHIELD.

”

MORIHEI UESHIBA

ago, a month ago, five years ago, or ten years ago. You'll be left in the dust if you do.

You're going to go through setbacks and crashes; and through every single one of those turns, it is up to you to find the answer. You have to be a person who can figure things out—that starts with being proactive. You cannot run from problems. No one will be there to save or protect you. You're alone in finding and creating solutions to the problems you face. Sometimes you'll get it right, and sometimes you won't. Sometimes it takes a few attempts to get it right. And sometimes, your solution will be to call on someone else for help.

While I was pledging my fraternity during my freshman year in college, our pledge class was tasked with creating a new chant to be used by our fraternity at our football and hockey games, parties, and so on. I took the lead on this project, and when I presented my first draft, I was laughed at, ridiculed, and thrown out of the room by my pledge brothers. Rejection is never an easy pill to swallow, and in my frustration, that red beast made his way to my thoughts. He wanted me to quit, to pass the project to someone else. And it was tempting. I didn't want to embarrass myself. I went back to the drawing board and began my second draft with a simple slogan: *Strike hard, strike fast, all the rest will finish last.* Before continuing, I presented it to my pledge brothers again to receive feedback. They liked it and told me to keep going. After multiple attempts, I wrote what became the fraternity chant going forward. While at first I failed, I refused to give up.

There are techniques for recommitting yourself to entering beast mode every day. Most daily spiritual practices remind us about what is important and how to move forward with our goals in mind. Every morning, I start my day reading some proverbs. This allows me to align my heart and my soul with wisdom and knowledge, like splashing cold water on your face, but for your soul; it wakes me up and puts me in a good mood. This daily ritual is empowering and positive. I want a good business, a strong family, and I want to live a good life. In order to have it all, you have to be physically fit, mentally fit, and spiritually fit.

Identify your own spiritual practice, and make it a daily habit, whether it's yoga, Pilates, meditation, lifting weights at the gym, journaling, or going to church or temple. These are all forms of spirituality. Pick the ones that make you a better person.

I personally have a tough time with the classical method of meditation because my mind races. I've done yoga with my wife, and I've attempted to meditate in the past, but I struggle because my brain doesn't shut up. I recently found that lying down and focusing on my breathing for about ten or fifteen minutes before I start my day calms me for the battle ahead. I am a work in progress on meditation. I know I am not alone in this, so if you're like me who struggles with the standard definition of meditation, don't worry—there are many ways to meditate. The definition of meditation, to me, is a place where you find peace of mind. I, for example, find peace of mind when I work out. When I take my dog for a walk, we stop and sit on a bench looking out at the water, and take a few short moments to think, breathe in the air, and find gratitude. That is also a form of meditation. My best friend swears by meditating, and some of the most brilliant minds in the world do so as well. In fact, Josh Waitzkin, author of *The Art of Learning* (which I highly recommend), maintains that meditating is without a doubt one of the keys to many of the most successful people in the world.

Some people use yoga or Pilates as their form of meditation, especially since those practices emphasize the importance of breathing. Running is meditation for those who find clarity on their runs. I recently read a Tim Ferris (@timferris) blog post where he recommended the Five Minute Journal. Open the journal every morning, and it begins with a quotation. It then prompts you to jot down what you're grateful for and what your goals are for the day. Before going to bed, it wraps up your day by asking you what you accomplished. Give yourself a few moments in the morning and at night to think, reflect, and write. This also works as a tool to look back and see how far you've come in different stages of your life. The takeaway here is to find what works for you and create a daily habit doing it.

Don't take what you have for granted. Walk around where you live and appreciate everything every day. Be grateful for what you have, not worrying about what you don't have.

You have to coach yourself in the morning to prepare for your day.

INTERVIEW WITH BARRY LEWIN

I first met Barry on the tennis courts at Williams Island in Miami, a place we both call home. After that we didn't see one another for quite some time, but we reconnected at an event, and I noticed a completely new shredded version of Barry. We had previously only met in passing, but his energy was contagious and his attitude on life was inviting—you just wanted to get to know him—so I approached him and asked what his trick was in getting so lean. From then on, a special bond formed, and Barry would become one of my close friends. On any given day when Barry isn't traveling the globe overseeing one of the many hotels he manages or checking in on one of his investments properties, I can count on him for five hours of war on the tennis court or a five-mile walk. Barry is a beast in all he does, both in business and in life. He insisted this interview be conducted while walking the island. He had steps to take since a couple of friends were ahead of him on a Fitbit weekly challenge, and no one beats Barry in steps!

LO: *How and why did you change your eating habits and fitness routine?*

BL: A friend of mine told me to watch the documentary *Forks Over Knives* [*a documentary that researches what* *would happen if people switched from an animal-based diet to a plant-based diet*]. After that, I went cold turkey and converted to an Eastern plant-based diet, with fish. I changed my entire eating philosophy. I went from 185 pounds, eating whatever I wanted, to losing twenty pounds in the first six to eight months. I have stayed that way for two and a half years, so I believe 165 pounds is my natural body weight. My energy level, my endurance, my thought processes all changed for the better. I found that while changing my eating habits and diet, my body processes food much quicker. I realized I needed to eat more often and to carry nuts and other natural food supplements to keep my energy levels peaking. As far as fitness goes, I always worked out, going to the gym three to four times a week, playing tennis, et cetera. The Fitbit was equally life changing for me because I was able to monitor my activity. It forced me to do things I have never done before. For example, I now walk three miles to get my hair cut. I would never have walked there three years ago. In New York, where I do a lot of work and business, I constantly called upon cabs or Uber if I had to go from midtown to downtown, but I now walk those streets. I walk everywhere. I do everything by walking. If I need to go to the eighteenth floor, I will often walk up the stairs and for sure walk down. I am so much more active than I ever was. Being a competitive individual, the Fitbit also gave me the ability to befriend a social group to participate with. If I knew Lonnie walked fifteen thousand steps, I wanted to walk sixteen thousand steps. And I think that is a life lesson for our kids and for us: When you compare how you are doing with a group you are competing with, it will elevate you. We hunt better when we are in groups. You want to be part of a group that can help support you, push you, and motivate you. It is part of human nature. I think the Fitbit was better than anything else on the market for that sole reason—its community. I use that philosophy in all my businesses I am involved with, too. Eating healthy and being active in unison is what got me to a place mentally where I feel so good all the time.

LO: *Do you run into people who say what you're doing is not healthy?*

BL: Sure, I get people who tell me not to get any skinnier, but I am not trying to get skinny! You have a lot of people who say they don't believe in my diet. "Where are you getting your protein? It's not good for you." But I don't really care. I am not trying to push my diet on anyone else. If someone is eating steak, great. I don't care what they eat. But if someone asks me about my diet, I will share it with them. They usually ask me if it's difficult. Anything is difficult at first, but once your body gets accustomed to it, it's not so difficult. It becomes mind over matter.

LO: *How did you end up in the hospitality business?*

BL: I graduated from Cornell in hospitality business in 1985. I interviewed with a bunch of companies, and I liked the entrepreneurial spirit of Hyatt. My dad was at a very senior level at Hilton at the time and really wanted me to go work there, which was not something I really wanted to do. I also have two older brothers who graduated from Cornell's hospitality school, and they both went to work for Hilton at the time.

LO: *So what did you do? Did you take the easy route, or did you decide to take the harder route?*

BL: I wanted to prove I could do it. I never wanted anyone to say I achieved what I did because of my father. I didn't resent my father or anything. I just wanted to do it on my own. I got hired to work at Hyatt and began as a management trainee with six hundred others where 50 percent survive. You work at every department for a year and learn the hotel management business at Hyatt. I worked in a nine-hundred-room hotel in Houston, Texas, during the downturn of the oil debacle. I became the assistant to Ron Day—who currently works for me. He was the executive steward at the time. I came in everyday at 5:00 p.m. and worked until he came in at 7:00 a.m., when I did turnover with him. I would work from 5:00 p.m. to 7:00 a.m. six days a week, sometimes seven, but I loved what I did. There was no five-day workweek. You worked and took time off if you had to. I did that until an opportunity came up for a position in sales. I was offered that job and did that for about eight months. Soon after, another sales position opened in the largest hotel Hyatt Regency has in Chicago. David, who was my manager, recommended me for the job. I was hired for that position and moved to Chicago, where I exceeded every goal and did extremely well. The regional vice president of Hyatt, Don Daporta—a legend at Hyatt and a real bigger-than-life kind of guy—took notice of me. We were at a management meeting, and he took me aside and asked if I could be resident manager of this hotel (one level below general manager). This caused some waves as I jumped a lot of people with more experience. The looks on some of the people's faces in the room who were slated ahead of me were not good. It shook some trees.

LO: *Why do you think Don Daporta took notice of you?*

BL: I would say it was personality, a combo of how my peers perceived me, my ability to work well with the customers of the hotel, and my knowledge of general hotel operations. Most people in sales never did operations. I had experience in operations and also happened to be good at selling, and Don felt those were attributes the hotel was lacking. I was someone who came in earlier and stayed later than everyone. When you combine all those different things, you increase your odds of getting noticed.

LO: *When do you end up going off on your own?*

BL: I stayed with Hyatt from 1985 to 2004. I left Chicago in 1989 for Puerto Rico, then to Hawaii, and my first general manager job was in Palo Alto, California, in 1993. I lived in a hotel from 1993 until 2004. It was great and a lot of fun. I left Hyatt in 2004 and worked for Blackstone through an acquisition. In 2012, Prospect Hotel Advisors was created as the expert in operations of hotels in which 80 percent of what we did was for Blackstone. We essentially served Blackstone. We advised on assets we owned, allocated capital, made sure the hotels were operating at their highest efficiency, got the greatest returns on investment, and also looked at new potential assets to acquire.

LO: *With all this activity, how many hours of sleep do you get a night?*

BL: Five to six hours is what I need. With my travel schedule, I will sleep on the plane and nap if the environment allows it. I'm a big fan of quick power naps and usually get them in on the weekend.

LO: *What's the most important character trait you look for in others?*

BL: People who are humble, can listen, have good character, and who are honorable and trustworthy. I think if you tie those altogether, you would call it integrity.

LO: *When I say the word* beast, *what pops into your mind?*

BL: Aggressiveness. Someone who is determined to achieve the goals he or she sets for himself or herself.

LO: *What advice do you have for someone who is stuck or down on his or her luck?*

BL: If you're not happy in your situation, it is up to you to change it. You need to look at the bright side of that situation and deal with it. If you can do that, it will turn around.

Barry is a ball of energy. Whether he is running to one of his three daughters' volleyball games, walking around the island, playing tennis, overseeing a new hotel, or chasing down deals, his heart operates at 110 percent. I'm glad to have this beast in my corner.

CHAPTER 7

THINKING LIKE A BILLIONAIRE AND CREATING YOUR OWN MAGIC

"Big shots are only little shots who kept shooting."

CHRISTOPHER MORLEY

Your mentality, your positivity, and what you put out into the universe are huge components to your success in life. People underestimate the power of positive thinking and the power of visualizing success. This chapter is about the power of your mind, thinking positively, and getting your finances right. You are capable of creating your own magic.

You've probably heard people say, "If you can see it, you can achieve it." Well, there's a reason for that. Mental imagery, or visualization, is one of the most powerful skills you can use to enhance mental toughness and performance. Research has shown that if you prepare mentally and believe you can accomplish a task, you will increase your chances of success. If you allow negative thoughts and doubts to enter in, they will decrease your chances of success. You become what you think. It's during times of great struggle where positive thinking can be a game changer. Focus on the things you can control, and believe in yourself.

We've covered in a previous chapter the importance of writing down your goals, but it bears repeating. The power of the pen and putting it down on paper is unlike anything I've ever experienced. Do not cheat yourself by thinking you have everything "noted" in your head. Write it down! Think big, but start small. While your dreams should be huge, you start by getting that first small deal, that first client; then the momentum starts to build. It is important to realize this. People like to talk about all the big-ticket items or sales, but don't let that discourage you. Most billionaires started with a small deal that led to another decent deal, and so on. No matter what it is, if you want something and you're passionate about it, you are capable of achieving it.

off for a year or two, keep going. It might take a few more years for something to come along, or it might happen tomorrow. Keep working your ass off so you get noticed as someone with grit, perseverance, and persistence.

With that being said, plenty of goals won't pan out, and that's normal. Don't let this discourage you. As we grow and change in life, our goals will change, too. Situations out of your control can alter everything you've worked for, and how you handle such events is in your power, so focus on that. My goals today, as a married man and father, are much different than when I first started in the business. In fact, my goals change constantly because I'm always striving for improvement and I'm always challenging myself. Your goals can change by the year, by the month, or by the day. The twenty-two-year-old trainee is a completely different person than the forty-one-year-old fee-based financial advisor sitting in the office. So much in business has changed over the years, and it's constantly evolving. Like a tree in a storm, either you bend with the wind or you snap.

I often find myself thinking about the individuals about to start the New York City marathon. Every one of those people is a beast because of what it takes to get to that starting line. Even if a runner doesn't make it to the finish line, she is a beast because she tried, and more likely than not, she trained for several months or years beforehand. These runners pushed themselves outside of their comfort zones to accomplish something they didn't think was possible.

Look at the greatest jiu-jitsu masters. They all started as a white belt. After years of dedication and hard work, they achieved one of the highest levels of their vocation: a black belt. The vast majority of billionaires also started out as white belts in business and, overtime, achieved the highest levels of success.

Creating magic is about the law of large numbers. Your chances of creating magic increases the more you work, the more you put yourself out there, and the more you take yourself out of your comfort zone. It's all about maximizing your attempts at your goal and learning from each attempt. This can be applied to anything. If you're looking for a job and want to work up the corporate ladder, send your resume to hundreds of job openings and reach out to your contacts, friends, and relatives for help. In business, especially in sales, the law of large numbers is everything. I learned early on that it was a numbers game. When I increased the amount of contacts I made, I garnered more clients. The more I heard "no," the closer I was to getting a "yes."

In addition to working his ass off—whether in the gym, at the office, or at home—a beast always keeps track of his energy. I've noticed in my own life that money is energy.

“

IT ALWAYS SEEMS IMPOSSIBLE UNTIL IT’S DONE.

”

NELSON MANDELA

When I have my finances in order, everything else seems to flow much smoother. I enjoy whatever I am doing more without the stress or headaches of financial instability. For some people, talking about money is taboo and has a negative connotation—and I don't get that. We're all working toward making more money in our lives so we can have more energy to do the things that are necessary (taking care of family) or to do the things we want (vacation, travel, give to charities). People want to shy away from talking about money, but money is important. We live in a society where the dollar is king, so why do we shy away from talking about it? You need it to live. You need it to eat. You need it to do the things you love. You're going to need it to accomplish some (if not all) of your goals. You need it to buy the best equipment for your job because you'll need the highest quality and most innovative technology to stay ahead of the curve. Remember, you are the CEO of your brand; invest in that brand.

Once you're in a good place physically, emotionally and spiritually, you'll start accumulating wealth. Perhaps money scares you, confuses you, or makes you nervous because you're unsure of what to do with it. Allow me to outline some basic, common-sense solutions to get you started. Always consult with a professional when investing. If you have any questions, I can be reached at LinkedIn at Lonnie Gordon Ogulnick, at www.gordonwealth.net, by email directly at lonnie@gordonwealth.net, or by phone at 786-360-5023.

GORDON WEALTH TIP ONE

Spend less money than you make.

GORDON WEALTH TIP TWO

Invest the difference.

Those are the two fundamental keys to building wealth. Pretty simple, right? But let's take it a little further.

GORDON WEALTH TIP THREE

Take a piece of paper and draw a line down the middle. Write down all of your expenses on the left side—all of the money going out on a monthly basis. This includes monthly bills, mortgages, rent, car payment, credit card payments, loans, child care, groceries, gas, and so on. On the right side, write down how much money you earn *after* taxes. This is called your cash-flow analysis. You should have a positive number. If you don't, look at the list of expenses and find something to cut back on. Alternatively, you can also pursue making more money, and I highly suggest creating other income streams.

GORDON WEALTH TIP FOUR

Don't buy things you can't afford. That sounds simple, but most—if not all—of us have credit cards. Develop a habit of paying off any and all debt by the end of each month because interest rates on credit cards are high and painful. There are plenty of credit cards on the market that offer benefits with each purchase, but the most important rule you must instill in yourself in regard to any credit card is to pay off the entire balance at the end of the month. If you have a high balance and are unable to pay it off in one, swift swoop, create a plan to pay the balance down as quickly as possible to avoid paying interest rates over a long period of time. This might mean sacrificing spending money elsewhere, so don't get down on yourself if you can't take that fancy vacation yet.

GORDON WEALTH TIP FIVE

Build a war chest of six to nine months' worth of your monthly expenses in a savings account never to be touched except in emergencies. Things happen when we least expect it, so it's important to have a cushion. You will sleep better at night.

GORDON WEALTH TIP SIX

Whether you own your own business or work for a company, invest as much as you can in your retirement fund. The government likes to take your money! When it comes to retirement, Uncle Sam gives you a gift—and it's not often that Uncle Sam gives gifts. If you make $150,000 per year taxed at 28 percent, $42,000 goes straight to the federal government in taxes. If you put away $17,500 to retirement in one year, you will only have to report $132,500 to the government. That $17,500 will grow, tax deferred, and you will have saved $4,900 in taxes that you keep rather than pay to the government. You just got a guaranteed return of 28 percent on your money. That is a damn good rate of return that Uncle Sam gives you even before you invest it. If you work for a company that matches, take advantage of it. If you own your own company, you can put more money away per year (consult an advisor and or your accountant for a retirement plan best suited for your company). Pay yourself first. Think of investing in your retirement as a forced savings plan, and you will be comfortable in retirement. The earlier you start, the better.

GORDON WEALTH TIP SEVEN

Compounding interest is what Albert Einstein coined as the eighth wonder of the world. Compounding interest, in simple terms, is interest on interest. It is the result of reinvesting interest rather than paying it out so that money in the next period is then earned on the principal sum plus the previously accumulated interest. You may have heard the story about how the Native Americans sold Manhattan Island for twenty-four dollars. Sounds like a great deal for the buyer, right? If the Native Americans made an investment of that twenty-four dollars, however, and earned 8 percent annualized starting in 1626, 375 years later in 2001, they would have earned $82,000,000,000,000 (that's $82 *trillion*). According to a paper written by a trio of economists from Rutgers, the 2014 value of Manhattan Island was $1.4 trillion. Indians could have bought back Manhattan and gifted the 1.5 million people living there roughly $50 million a piece to find another place to live. Had the Indians understood the power of compounding interest, they would have gotten the better end of that deal. Men like Warren Buffet and Ben Franklin fully understood the power, and so can you. Assuming you save twenty dollars per day at a 10 percent compounding interest rate, you can grow $1.5 million in thirty years. If you are risky and can compound saving twenty dollars per day at 20 percent a year, then in fifty-four years you will be worth $1 billion.

GORDON WEALTH TIP EIGHT

Diversify and invest based on your own personal goals and risk, not some benchmark. Analyzing risk means asking, "What are the chances that this investment will go to zero?" Diversifying your investments helps alleviate those chances. Once you have your emergency fund and have maxed out on your retirement investing, you have the free will to play it safe or take some swings at higher returns. When it comes to risk, only play with what you can afford to lose.

GORDON WEALTH TIP NINE

Get a financial advisor. Trying to do it alone is like taking a pen to a sword fight. I love this proverb: "Like iron sharpens iron, so do two friends sharpen each other." Work with someone you like and trust. This person won't always have the answers—and if he tells you he does, that should be a red flag. A financial advisor will help you build a plan, and whether that plan is ultrasafe or very risky, you'll have a partner to talk to. Life changes, and you should have a financial life coach who can help you at every stage. Should I rent or own? What insurance do I need? Should I get a pre-nup? Estate planning? Divorce? 529 plans? Gift accounts? The list goes on and on. Your financial life coach is a huge asset.

GORDON WEALTH TIP TEN

While it may be fun to hear stories of overnight hits and big hedge fund bets, if you're thinking of striking it rich in a concentrated one stock bet, you're probably better off taking a few hundred or a thousand dollars to the casino and playing blackjack or poker. Investing is a long-term commitment filled with ups and downs. You can invest in a company, but like anything, give it time to grow, mature, and pay off. Some of those investments will pay you dividends (income) while you wait, like collecting two hundred dollars every time you pass "Go" on the Monopoly board. Other investments may offer you a much larger return based on growth potential. A well-devised plan and time will be your allies while investing.

CONCLUSION

If you build your brand correctly, it'll endure the test of time. You have to equate your brand with quality, positivity, courage, and honor. Your good name is everything. Once you establish your reputation, people will naturally gravitate to you.

Becoming a beast is a game that never ends, because you will never let it end. A beast concentrates everything within him—from the minute he wakes up in the morning to the minute he goes to bed at night—to give 100 percent of his potential to live a better life.

Once you enter this mentality, the seed gets planted, and it grows, like Jack and the beanstalk. It takes different forms and shapes, but from what I've noticed of beasts in general, their desires don't come from greed but from the desire to constantly WIN!

ABOUT THE AUTHOR

LONNIE GORDON OGULNICK provides clients access to a range of investment vehicles that are specific to their individual needs. Lonnie is happily married to his wife Dara and has two daughters, Leah and Ella. You can reach Lonnie directly on his website at www.gordonwealth.net, by email at lonnie@gordonwealth.net or by phone at 786-360-5023.

65863654R10113

Made in the USA
Charleston, SC
11 January 2017